IMAGES
of America

MARPLE AND NEWTOWN TOWNSHIPS

IMAGES
of America

MARPLE AND NEWTOWN TOWNSHIPS

Mike Mathis

ARCADIA PUBLISHING

ISBN 978-0-7385-5023-7

Published by Arcadia Publishing
Charleston, South Carolina

Printed in the United States of America

Library of Congress Catalog Card Number: 2007921766

For all general information contact Arcadia Publishing at:
Telephone 843-853-2070
Fax 843-853-0044
E-mail sales@arcadiapublishing.com
For customer service and orders:
Toll-Free 1-888-313-2665

Visit us on the Internet at www.arcadiapublishing.com

Contents

INTRODUCTION

The histories of Marple and Newtown Townships have been intertwined in numerous ways since they were founded in the late 1600s. Long inhabited by a branch of the Lenni Lenape Indian tribe, both municipalities were later inhabited by Quakers who had been subjected to harassment by the Church of England for failing to pay tithes and attend services. One of them was William Penn, who in 1681 obtained land that encompassed the state of Pennsylvania in payment for a debt owed to his father by King Charles II. Penn, best known as the founder of Philadelphia and as the namesake of Pennsylvania, gave settlers the opportunity to buy or rent land for farming; many who could not afford the price worked as servants to pay their passage to the new country. The names of the first families who settled in Marple and Newtown Townships are memorialized today as streets, schools, and subdivisions: Ellis, Langford, Stanfield, Worrall, Caley, and Lewis.

Marple and Newtown remained largely agrarian through the late 1800s. Mills and tanneries operated as well, and small villages where commerce was concentrated began to appear. Broomall became the crossroads of Marple; Newtown Square became the business center of Newtown. Both Marple and Newtown were noted for their clean water and pure country air. Children from Philadelphia were sent to summer camps and wealthy Philadelphians seeking to escape the summer heat built vacation homes in Florida Park. In the early 1900s, a trolley line was established along West Chester Pike between Philadelphia and West Chester. It connected the outlying countryside with the city faster than ever before and would eventually contribute to the suburbanization of Marple and Newtown. While both townships experienced some new home construction in the 1920s, it was not until the 1950s that subdivisions took off. Lawrence Park, Rose Tree Woods, Valley View Acres, and Echo Valley were some of the popular developments that drew families from Philadelphia who wanted larger homes and more land than the rowhouses in Philadelphia could provide. Today, Marple and Newtown Townships are mature thriving communities with a variety of housing, shopping, and recreational activities.

One

Early Beginnings

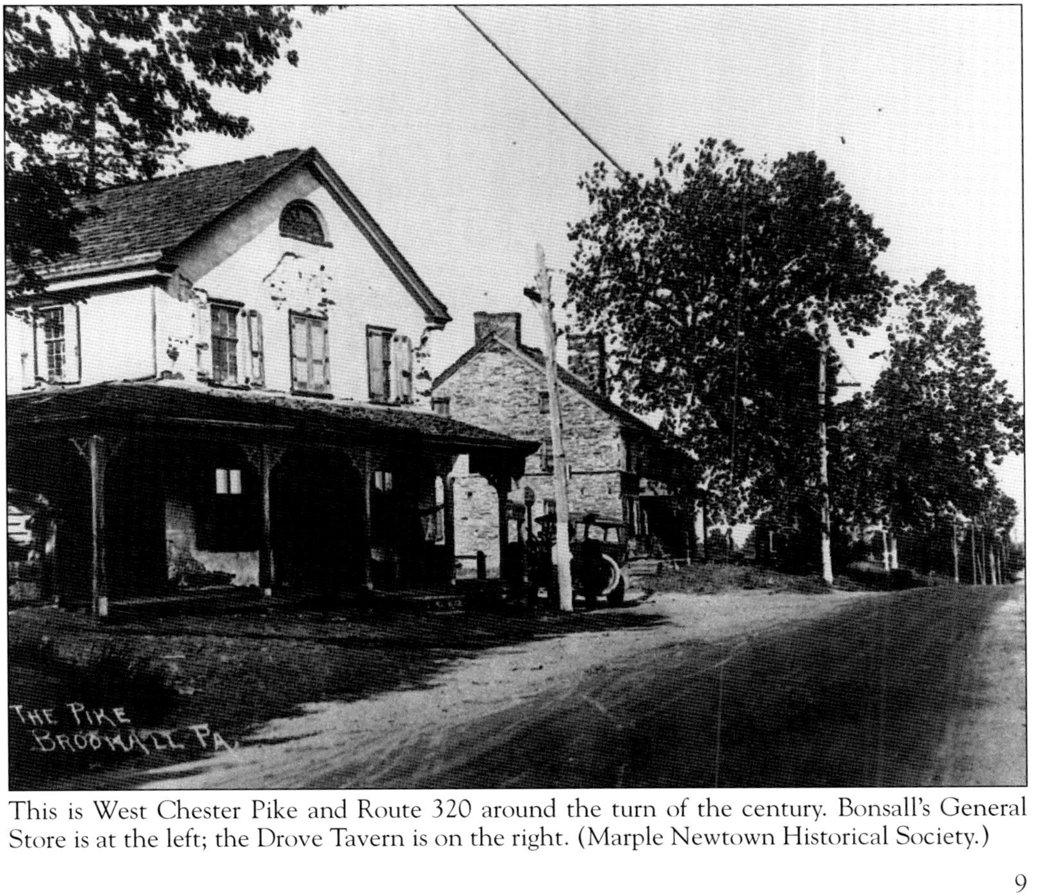

This is West Chester Pike and Route 320 around the turn of the century. Bonsall's General Store is at the left; the Drove Tavern is on the right. (Marple Newtown Historical Society.)

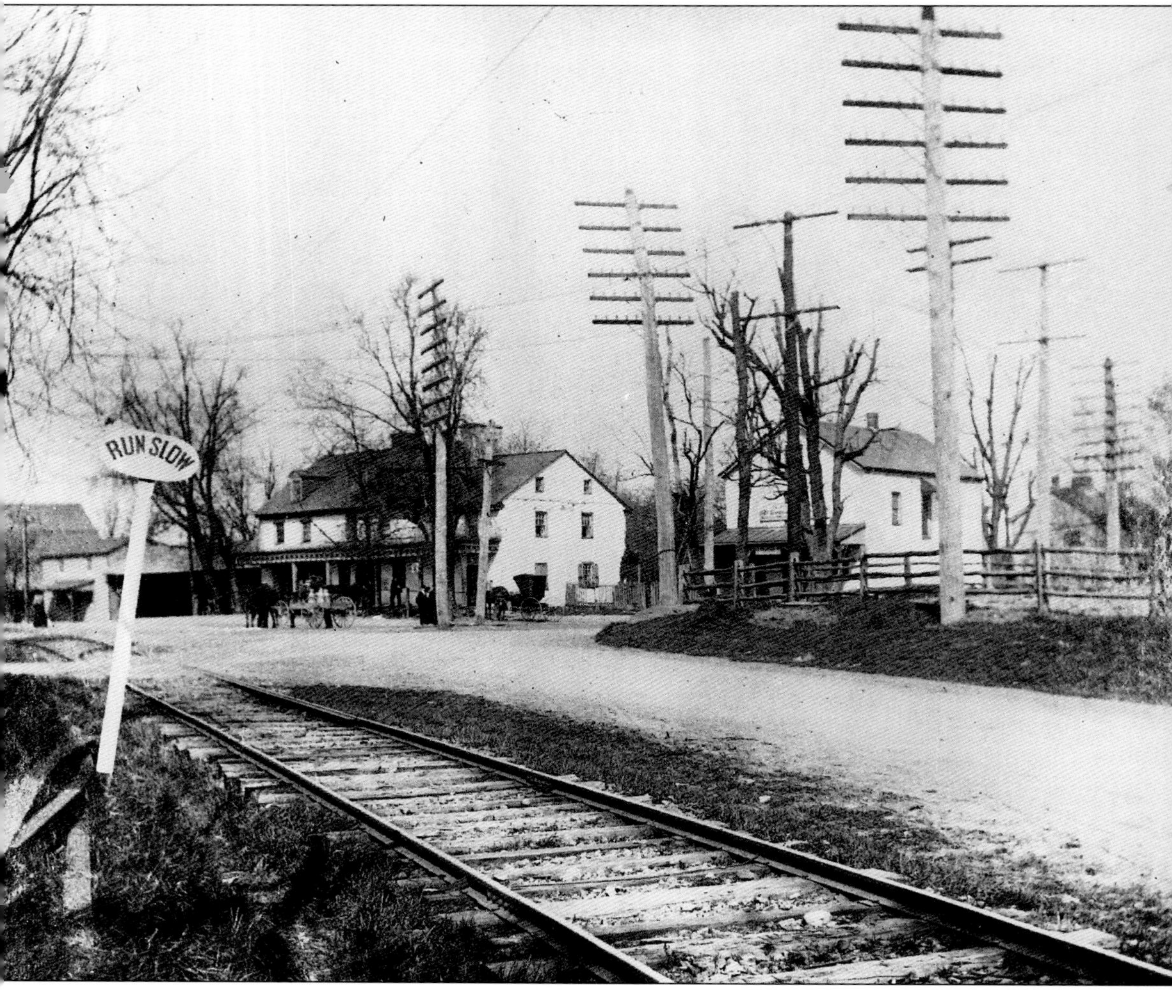

This is West Chester Pike and Route 252 around the turn of the century. (Marple Newtown Historical Society.)

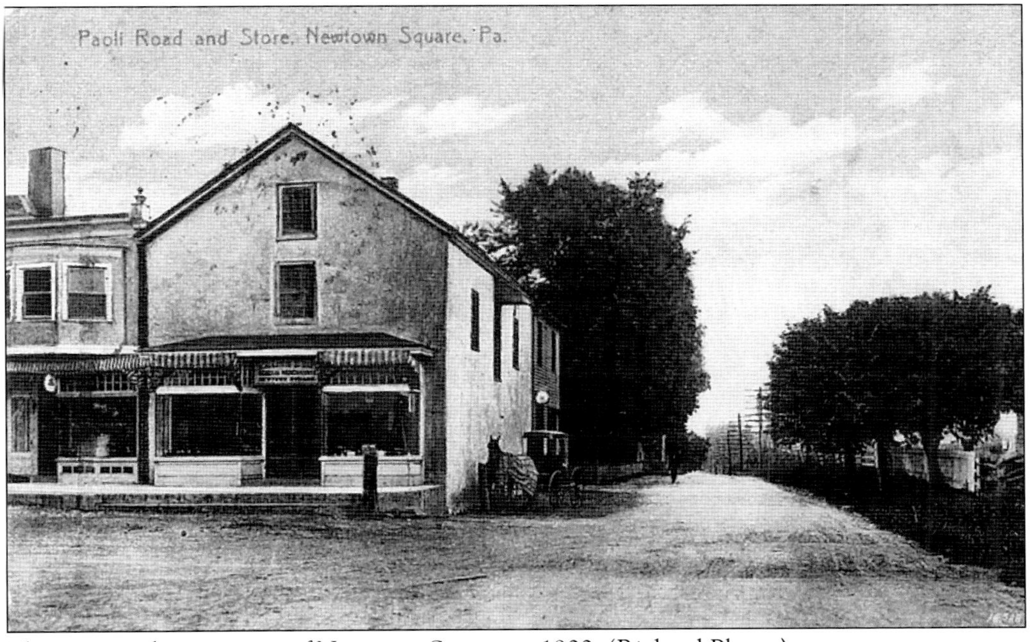

This is an early panorama of Newtown Square, *c.* 1900. (Richard Plotts.)

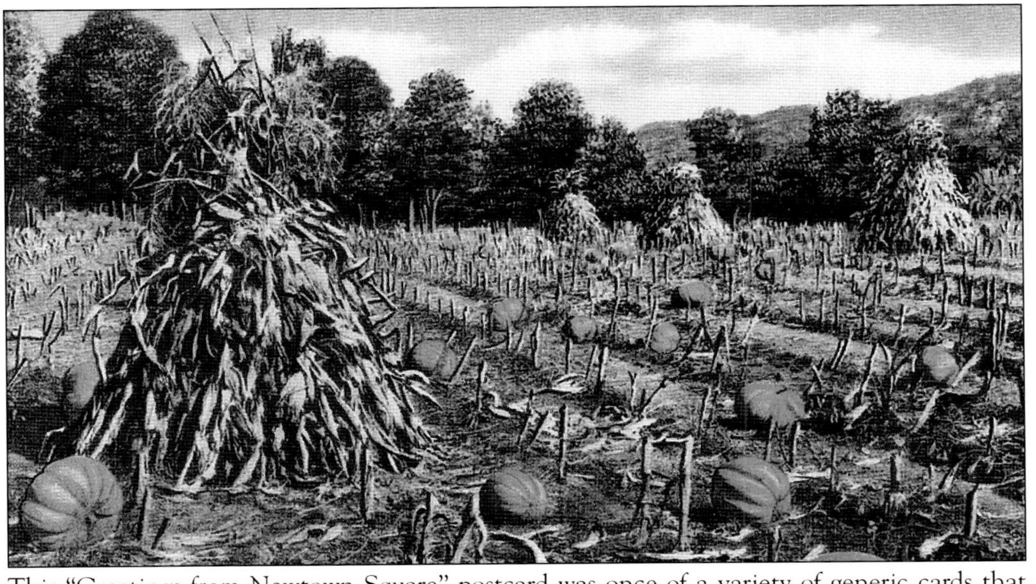

This "Greetings from Newtown Square" postcard was once of a variety of generic cards that travelers who passed through small towns were able to purchase at local stores around the turn of the century. (Richard Plotts.)

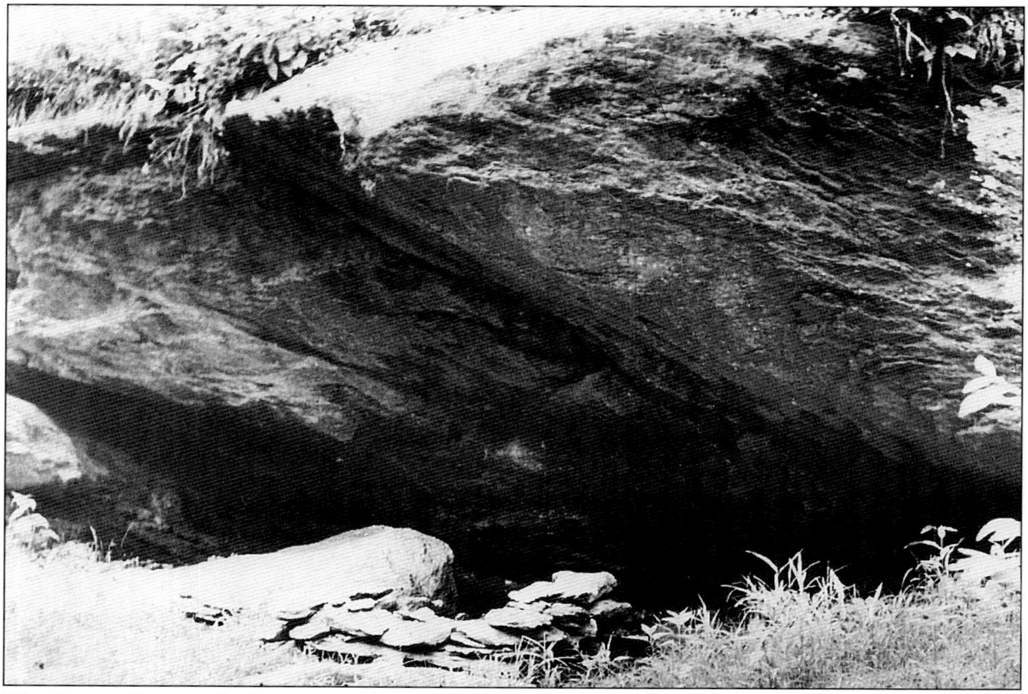

The Lenni Lenape Indian rock shelter on Langford Road near Lawrence Road was the site where, in 1940, archeologists discovered the remains of a Native-American woman whom they named Susie. (Marple Newtown Historical Society.)

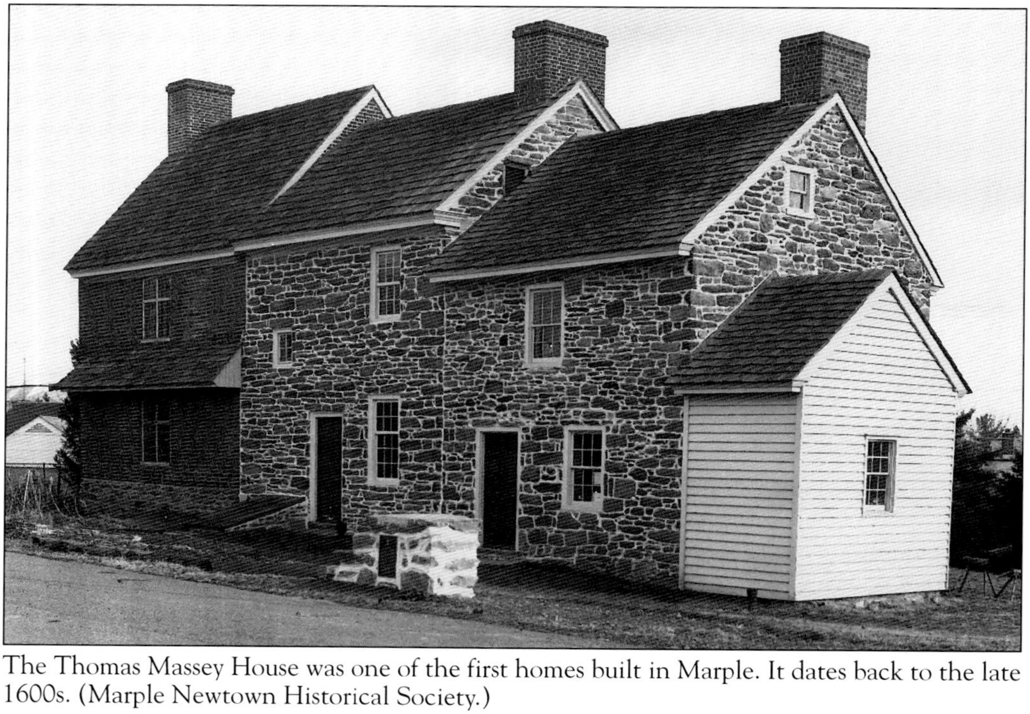

The Thomas Massey House was one of the first homes built in Marple. It dates back to the late 1600s. (Marple Newtown Historical Society.)

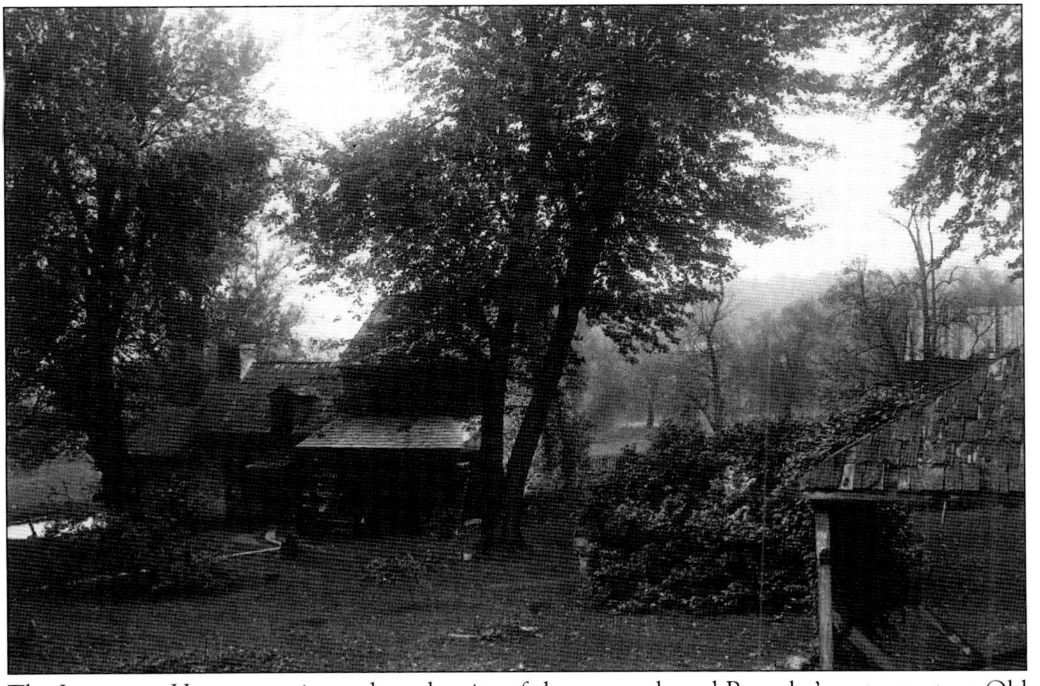

The Lawrence House was situated on the site of the car wash and Barnaby's restaurant on Old Lawrence Road. This photograph was taken in the early 1900s. (Hilda Lucas.)

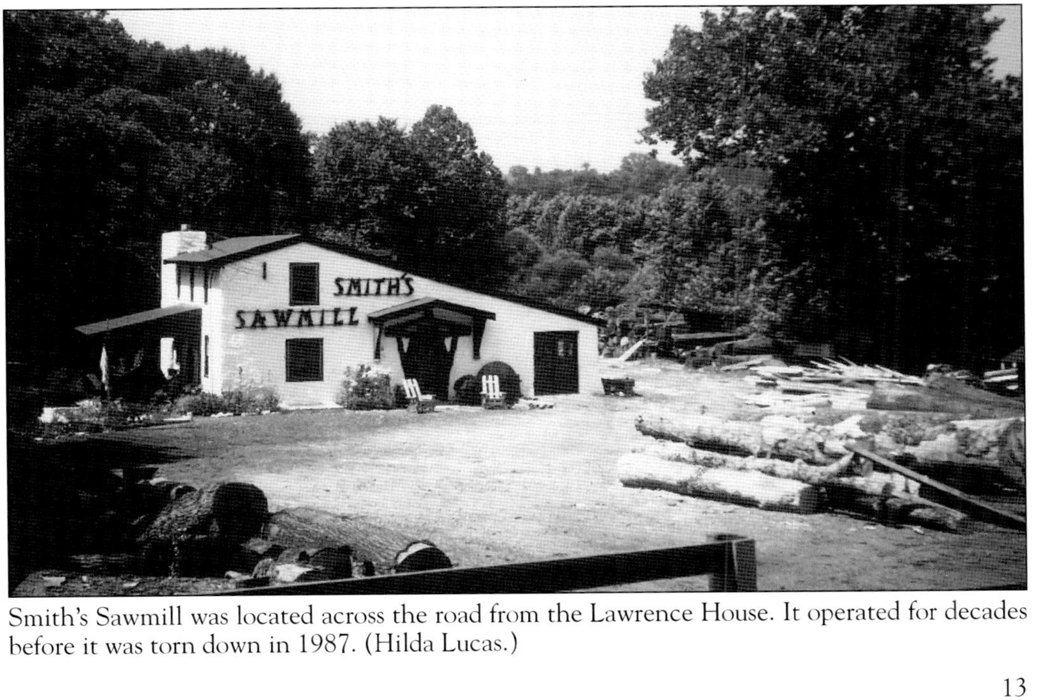

Smith's Sawmill was located across the road from the Lawrence House. It operated for decades before it was torn down in 1987. (Hilda Lucas.)

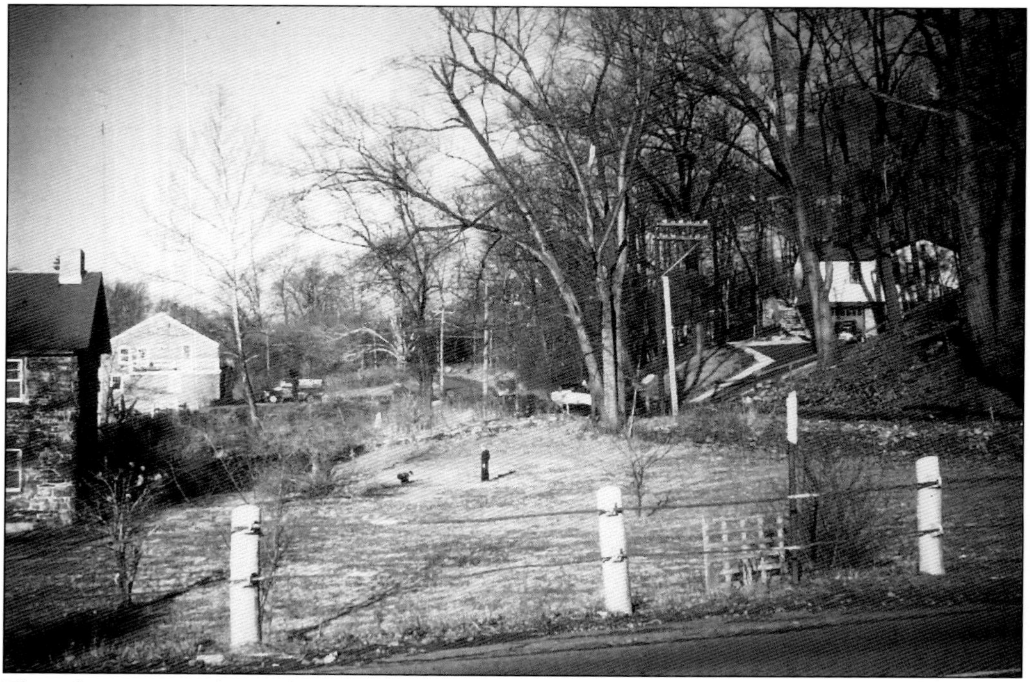

These homes were located on Old West Chester Pike near the Lawrence House and Smith's Sawmill. They were demolished to make way for Mercy Haverford Hospital. (Hilda Lucas.)

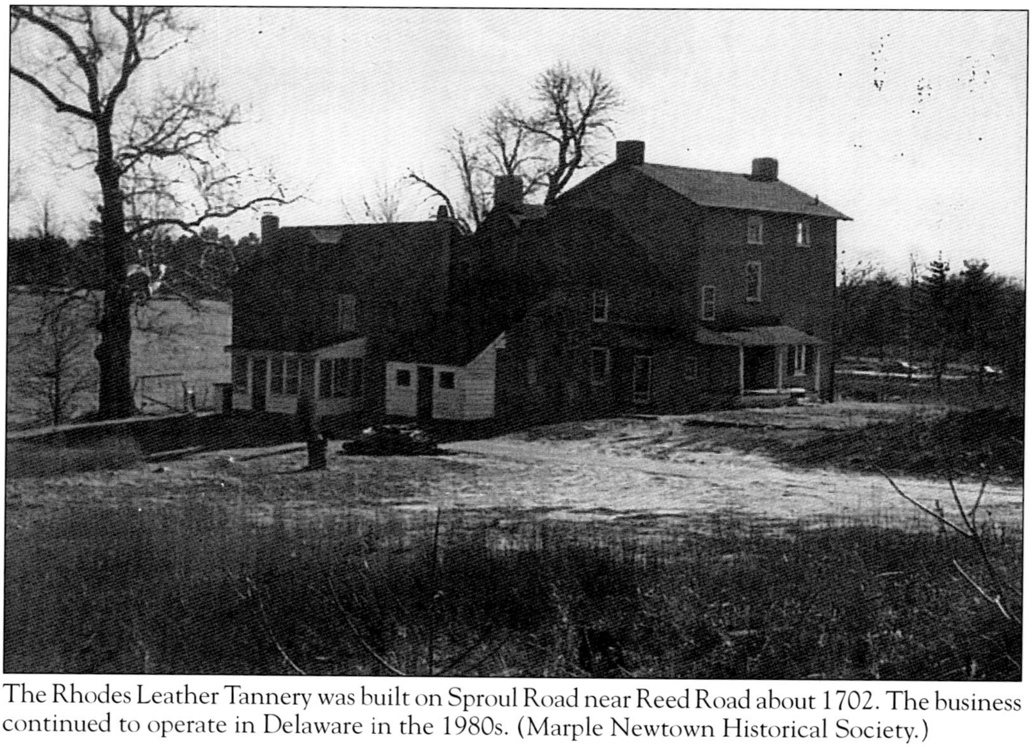

The Rhodes Leather Tannery was built on Sproul Road near Reed Road about 1702. The business continued to operate in Delaware in the 1980s. (Marple Newtown Historical Society.)

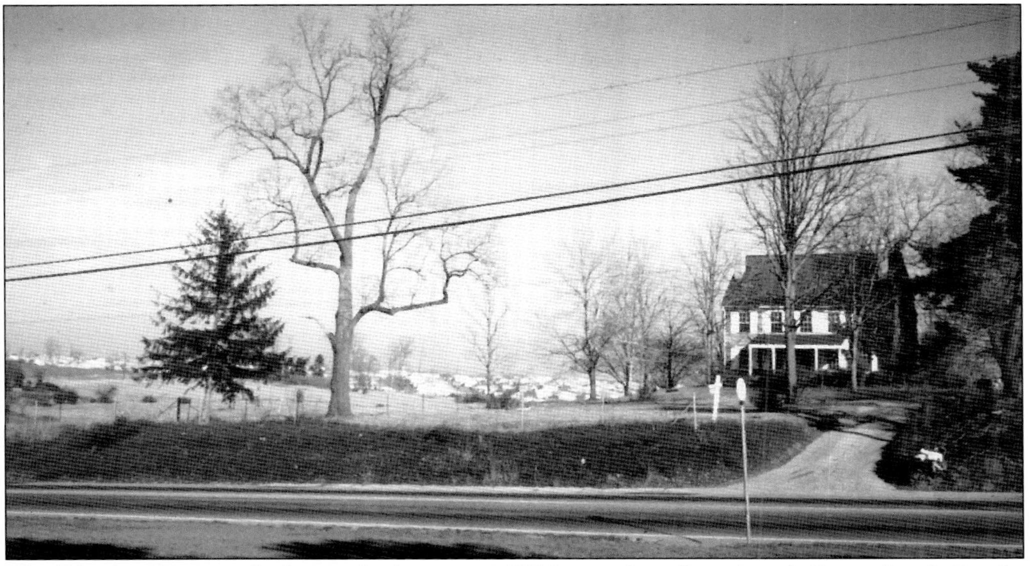

The Rhodes House, which was built around 1730, stood at Sproul and Crum Creek Roads. (Marple Newtown Historical Society.)

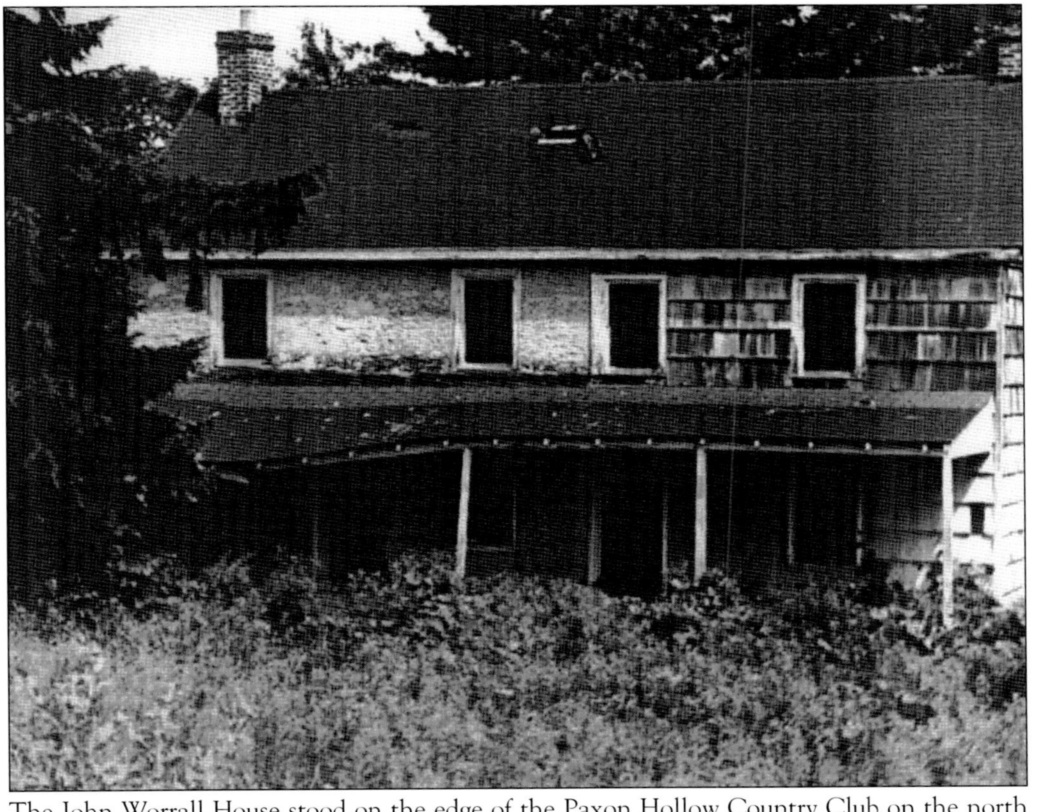

The John Worrall House stood on the edge of the Paxon Hollow Country Club on the north side of Palmer's Mill Road until 1960. The Martins Run home now stands on the site. (Marple Newtown Historical Society.)

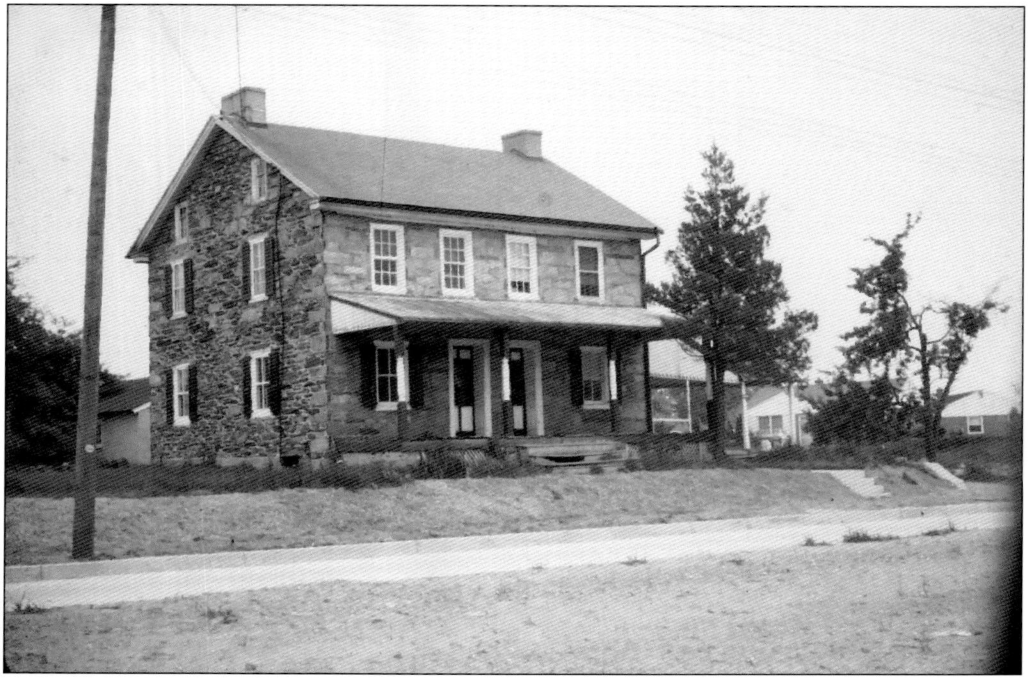

The old Culbertson farmhouse on West Chester Pike in Marple was the homestead of one of the area's longest-standing families. (Hilda Lucas.)

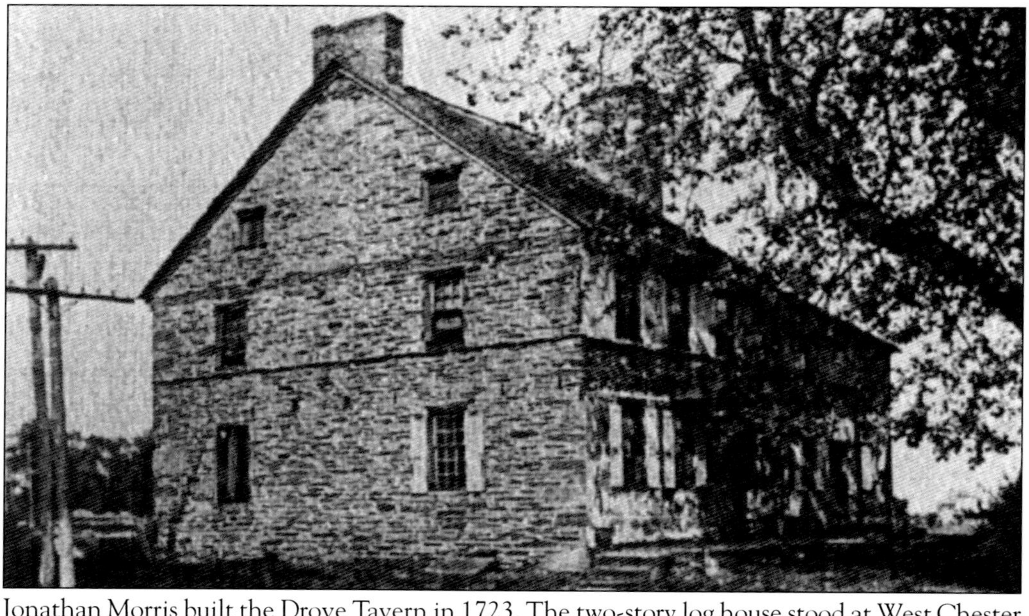

Jonathan Morris built the Drove Tavern in 1723. The two-story log house stood at West Chester Pike and Sproul Road for more than two centuries before it was demolished for the widening of West Chester Pike in the 1950s. (Marple Newtown Historical Society.)

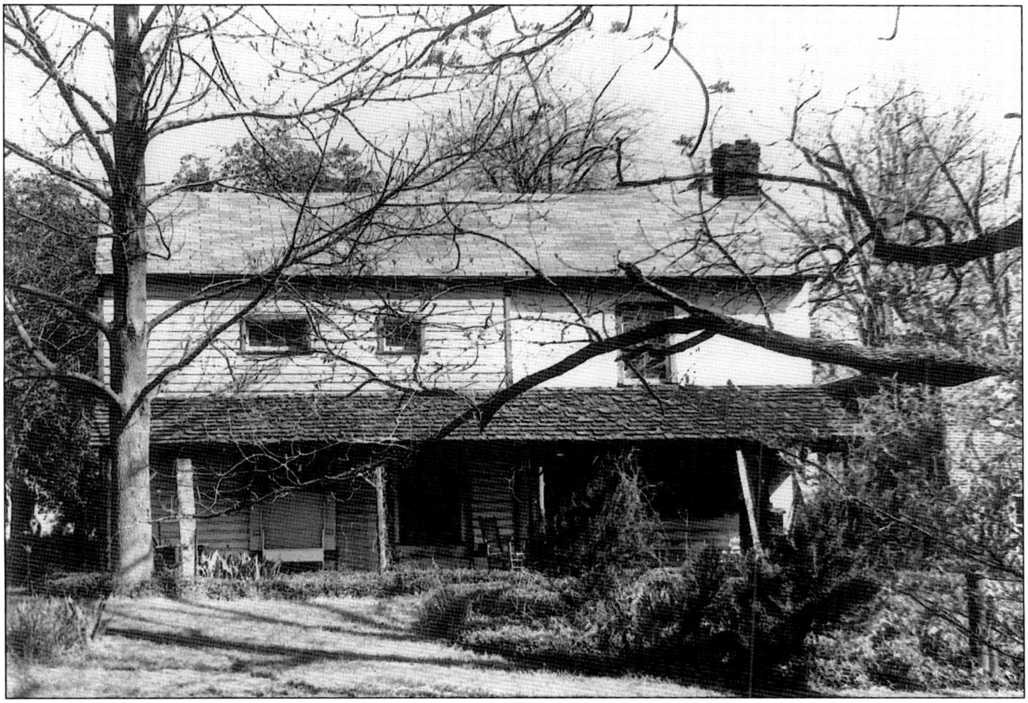

Highbriar on Langford Road served first as a permanent, and then as a summer, home for families through the 1950s. It was abandoned for years and is being restored by the Marple Newtown Historical Society. (Marple Newtown Historical Society.)

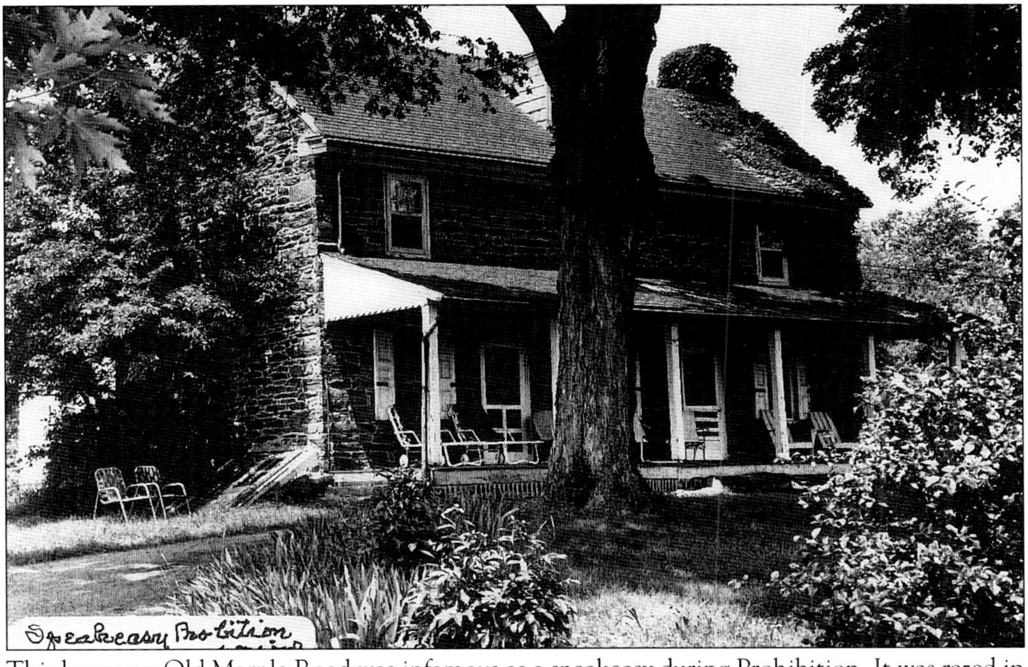

This house on Old Marple Road was infamous as a speakeasy during Prohibition. It was razed in June 1970 to allow the construction of the Marple Woods development. (Hilda Lucas.)

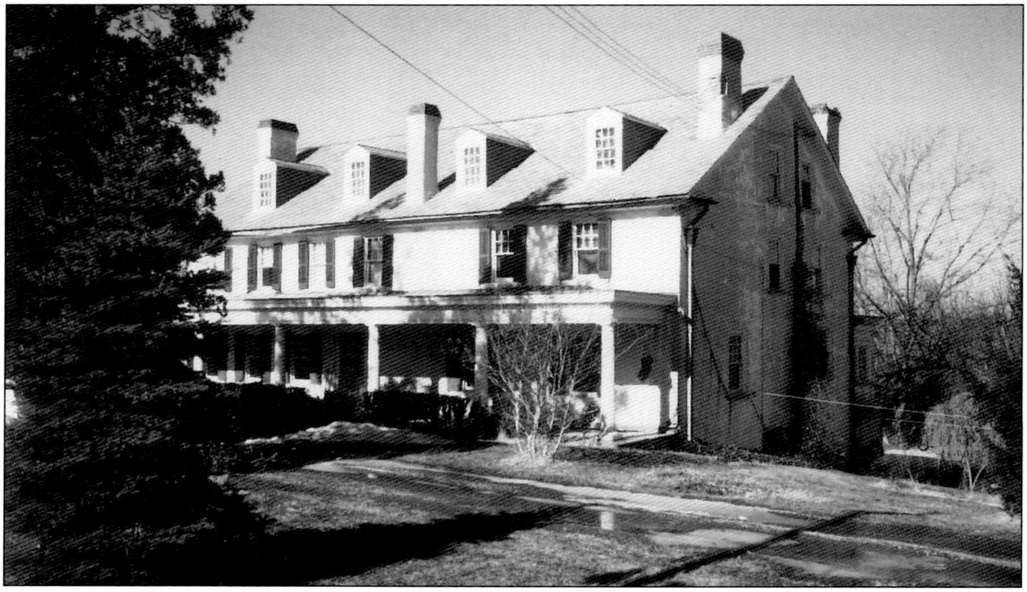

The Fox Chase Inn on West Chester Pike in Newtown was in business as an inn and stagecoach stand starting in 1727 and had been previously known as the Fawkes Tavern. It closed in 1870 and was converted into a private residence and later a business. (Hilda Lucas.)

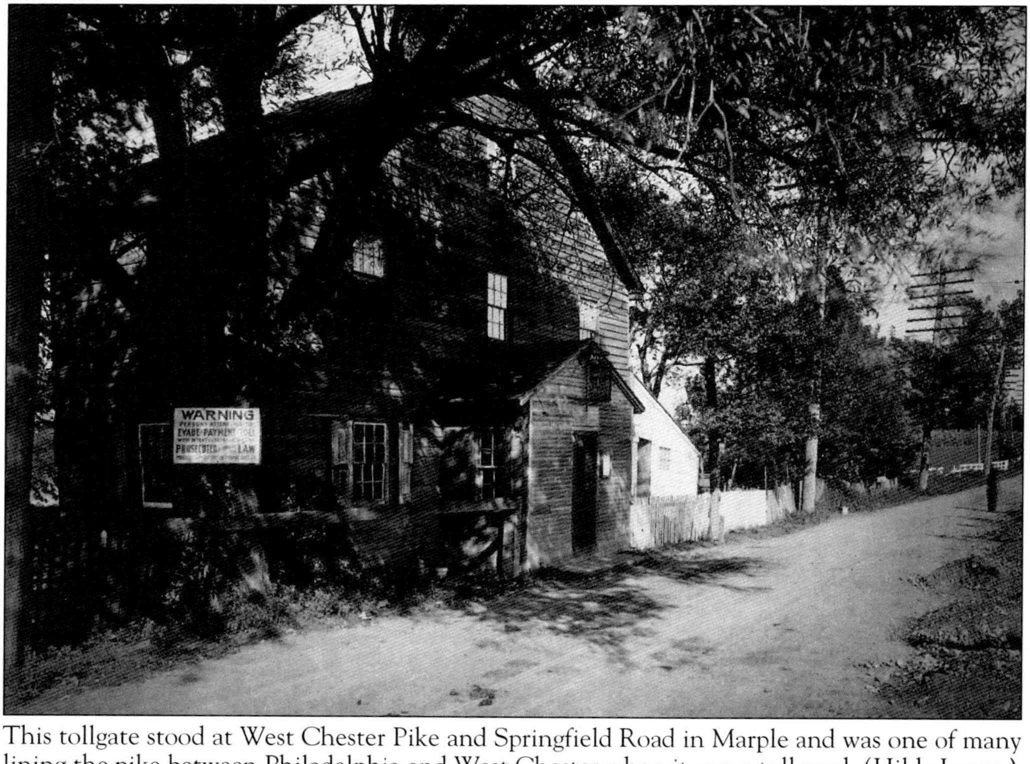

This tollgate stood at West Chester Pike and Springfield Road in Marple and was one of many lining the pike between Philadelphia and West Chester when it was a toll road. (Hilda Lucas.)

Two

Earning a Living

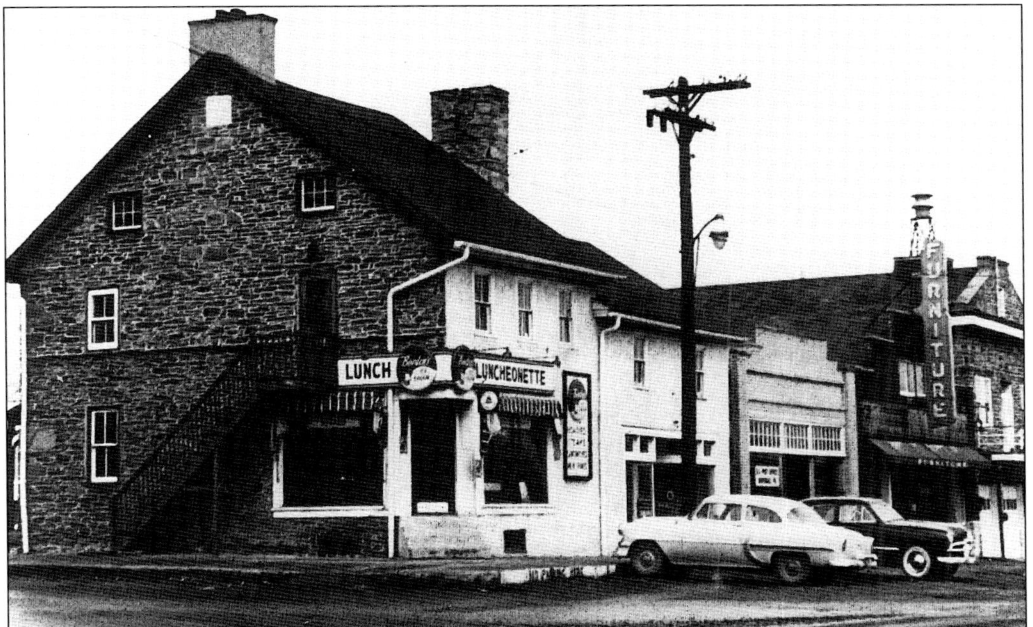

In later years, the Drove Tavern served as a corner store that operated under various names. It and two other buildings next to it were torn down when Route 320 was widened in the 1950s. (Marple Newtown Historical Society.)

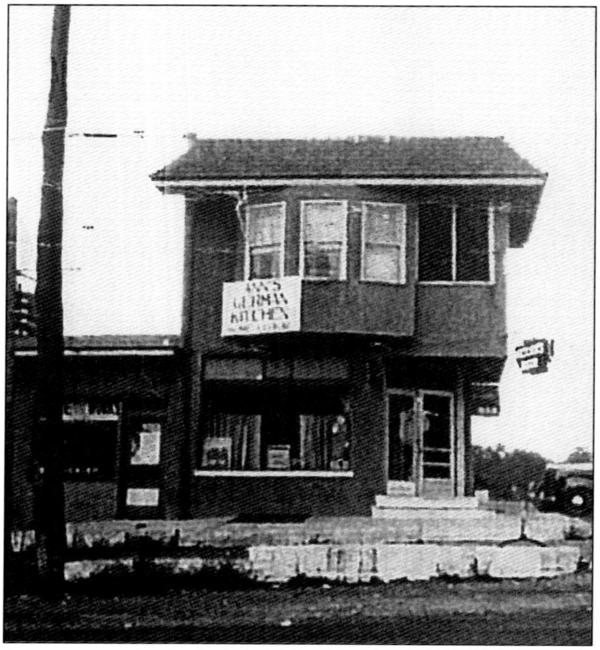

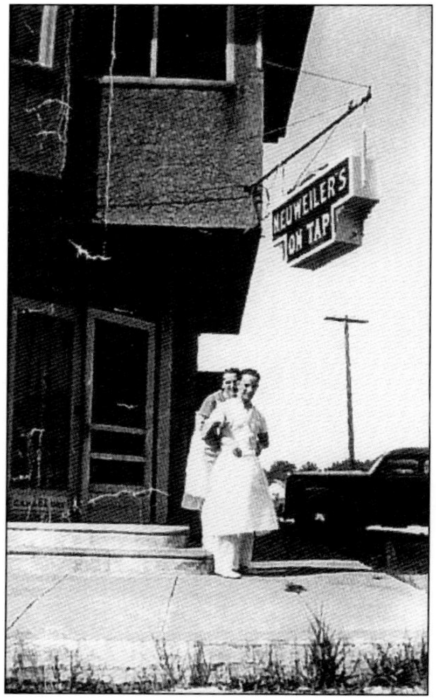

Many people believe Marple has always been a dry community, but Kurt Biebricher operated a tavern at West Chester Pike and Church Lane in the years after Prohibition. The township-owned Paxon Hollow Country Club now holds the only license in the township. (Dick Standen.)

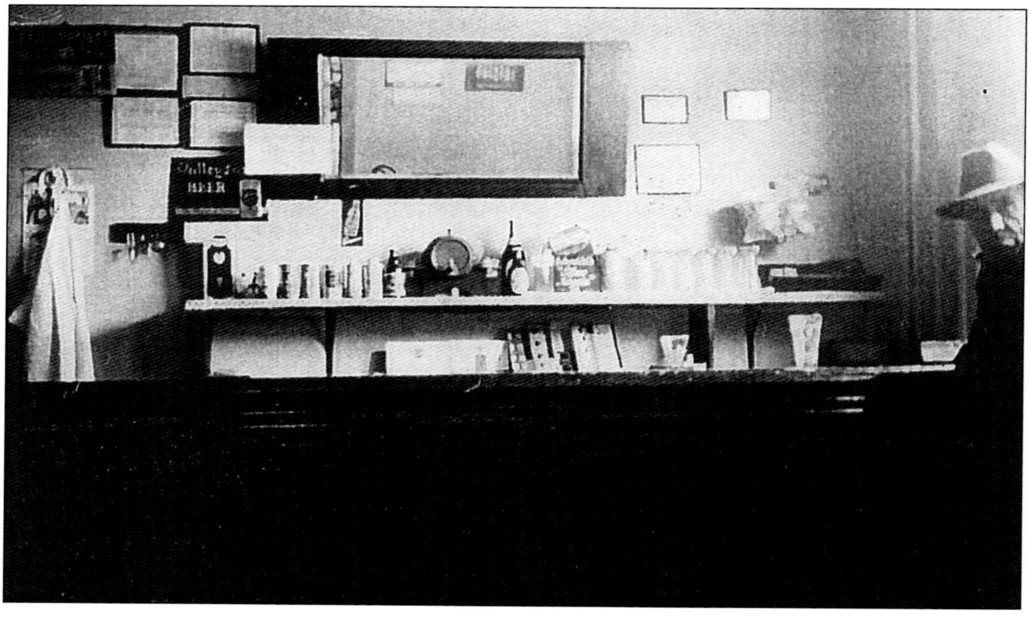

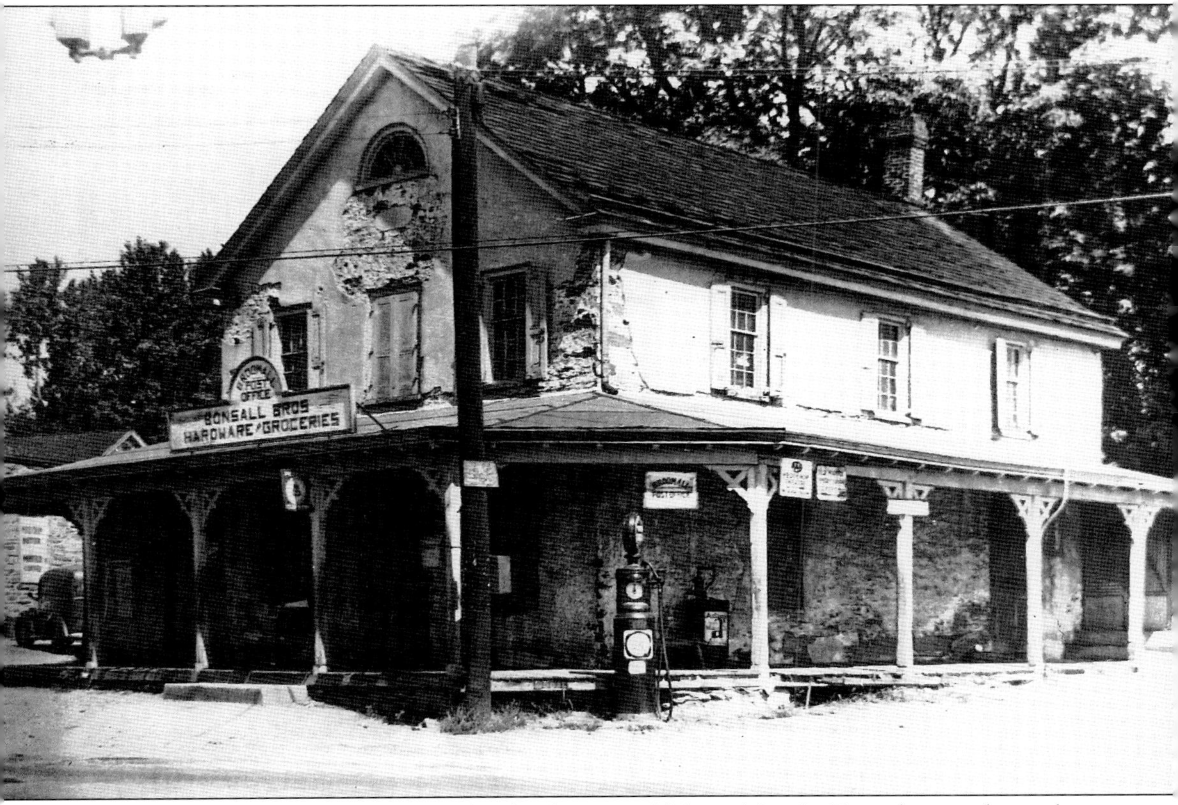

Bonsall Brothers General Store was the focal point of life in Marple Township in the early 1900s. It was where the train from Philadelphia delivered an array of items to the store and where residents gathered for a soda on a hot summer day. It also served as the Broomall Post Office. (Marple Newtown Historical Society.)

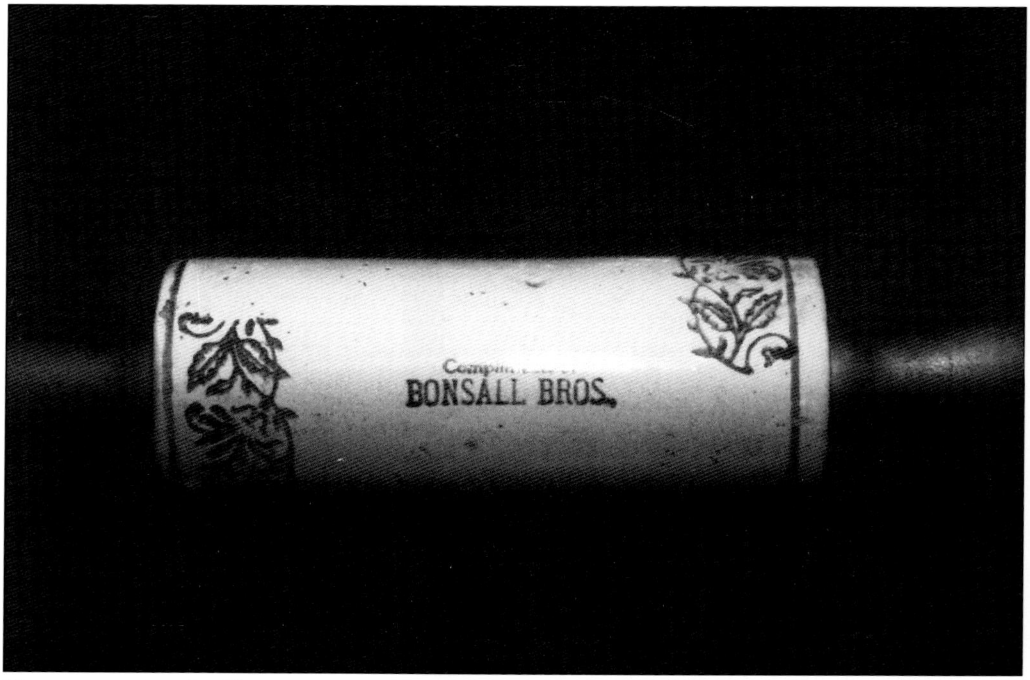

This promotional rolling pin was one of numerous promotional items that Bonsall Brother's General Store gave away to customers. (Mike Mathis.)

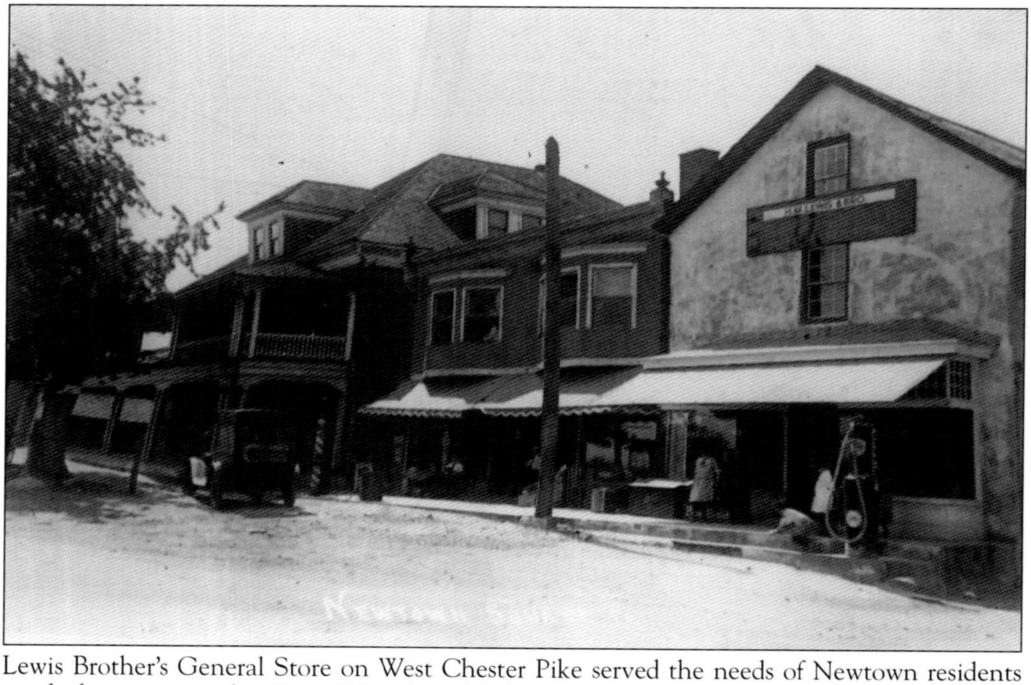

Lewis Brother's General Store on West Chester Pike served the needs of Newtown residents much the same way that Bonsall Brothers did for Marple residents. This photograph was taken in the 1920s. (Hilda Lucas.)

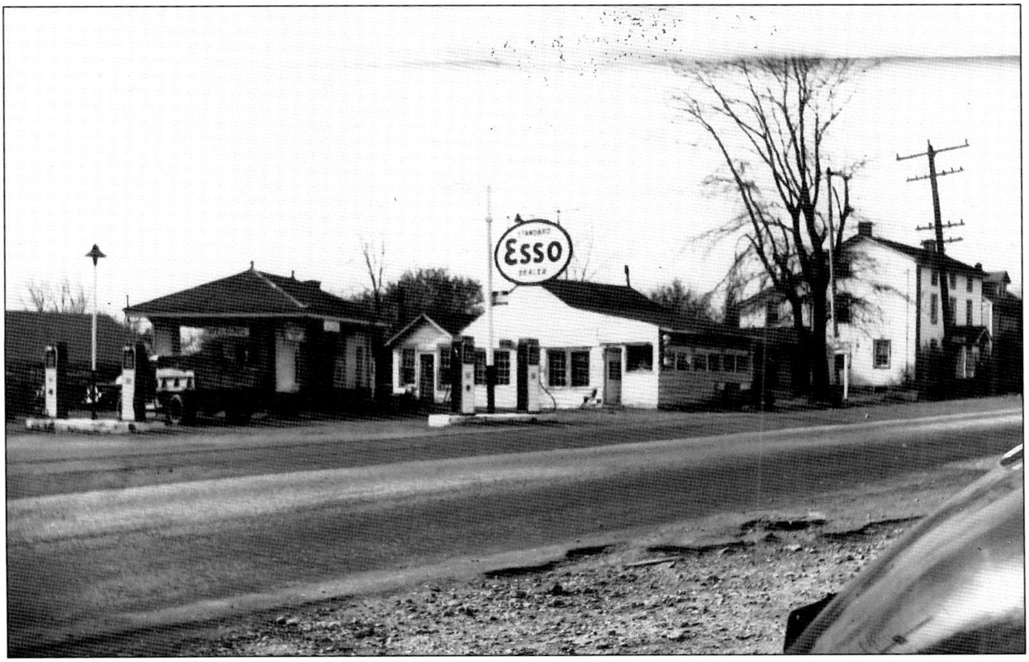

Eastburn's Esso was as much an institution and local gathering spot for early residents as Bonsall's store, which was located across West Chester Pike. (Al Vandetty.)

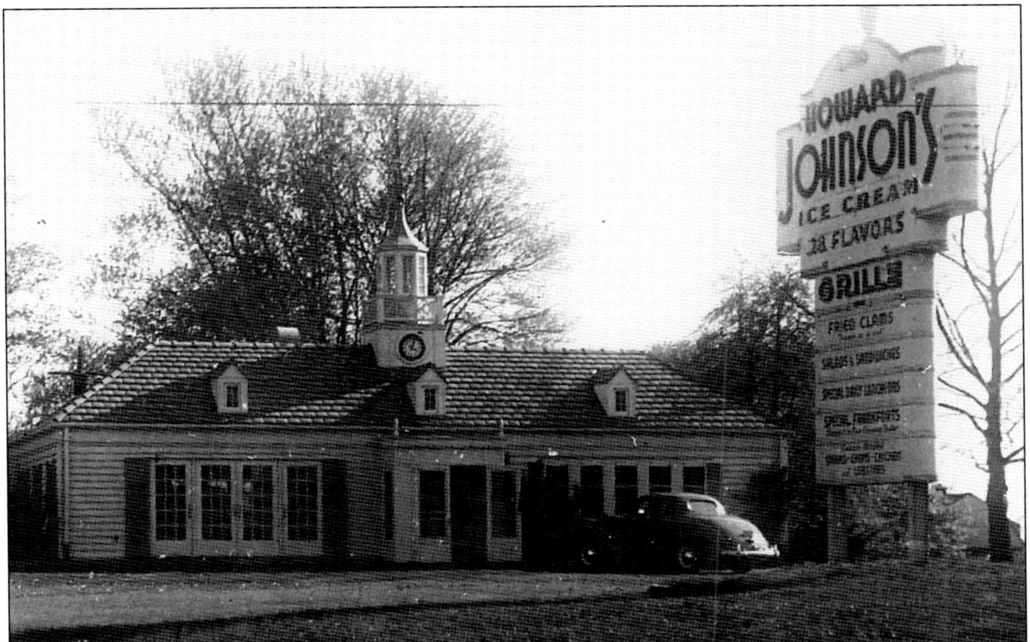

Long before the Country Squire served breakfast, lunch, and dinner to locals and travelers, Howard Johnson's stood on West Chester Pike in Broomall. (John Kuseian.)

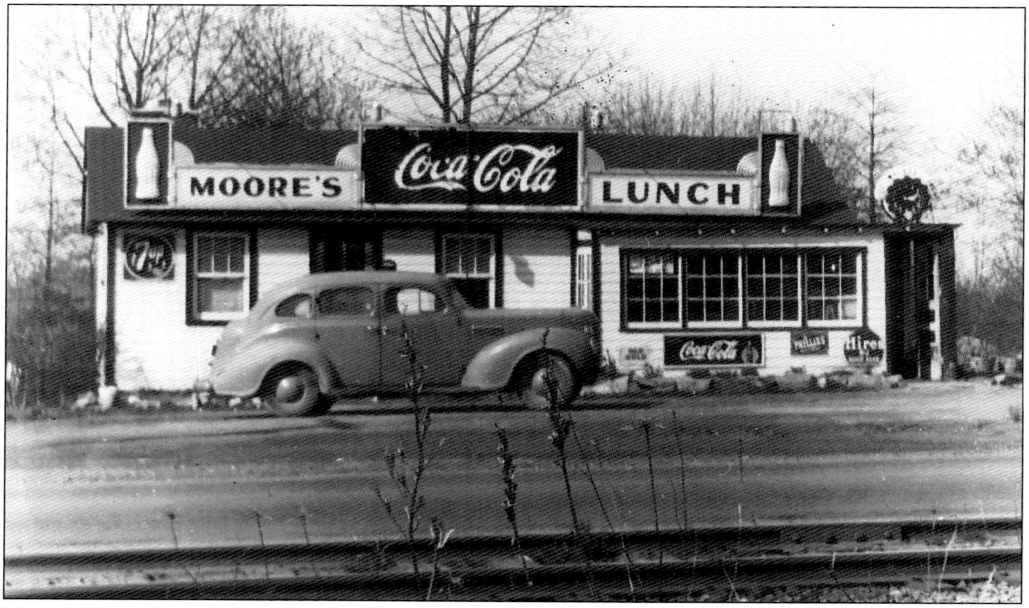

Moore's Luncheonette was one of several small restaurants that served residents and travelers between Philadelphia and West Chester in the 1930s and 1940s. (Al Vandetty.)

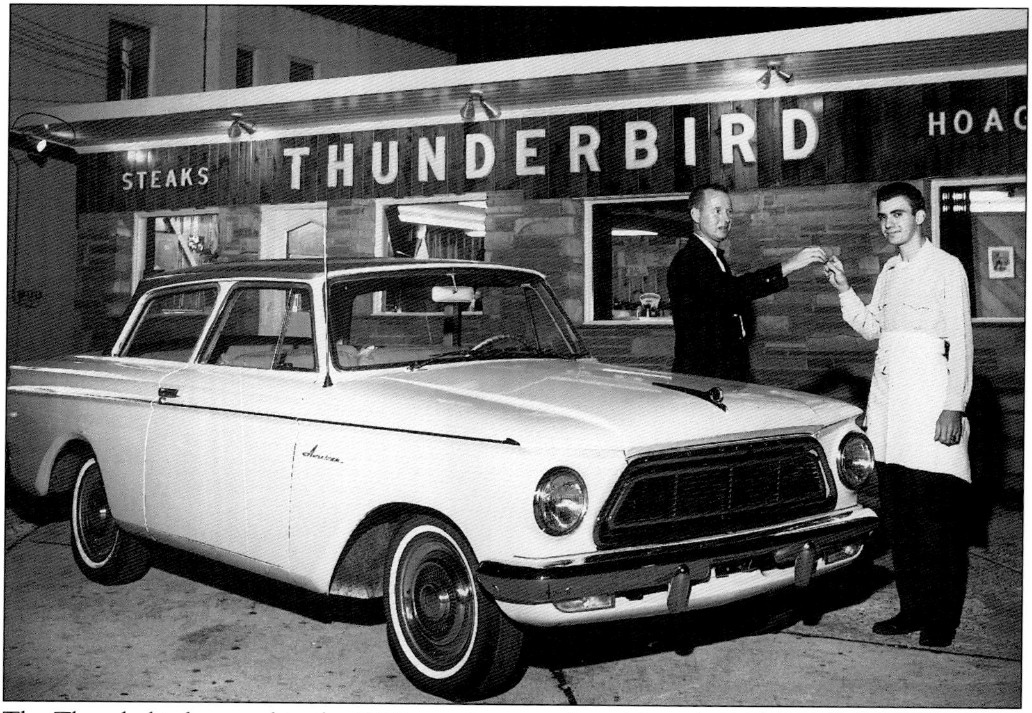

The Thunderbird opened in the 1950s on the spot where Moore's was located. (Bill Greco.)

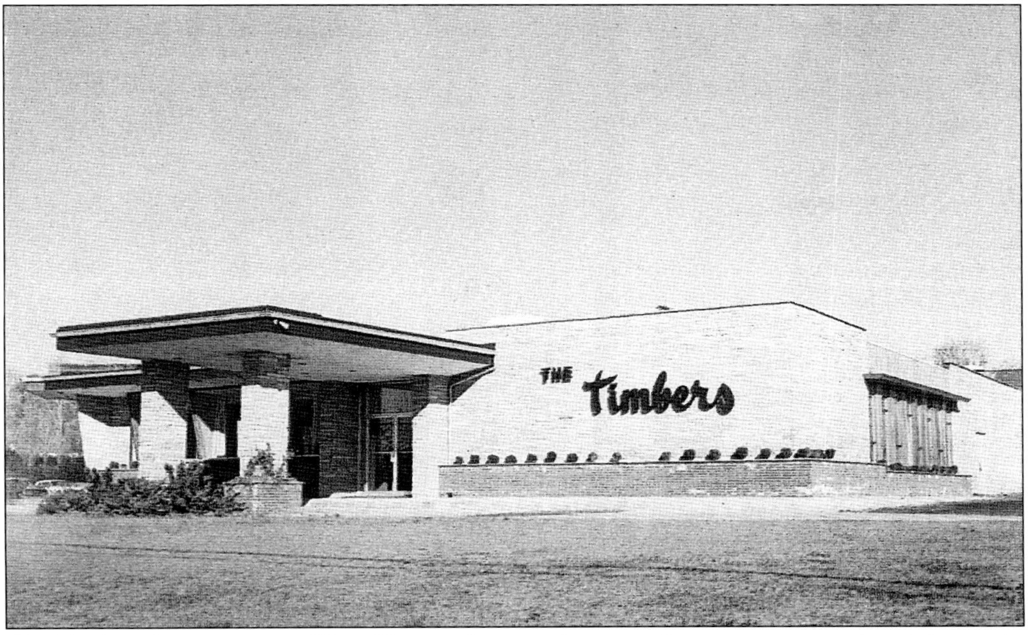

The Timbers Restaurant on West Chester Pike in Newtown Square was a popular nightspot in the 1950s and 1960s. (Richard Plotts.)

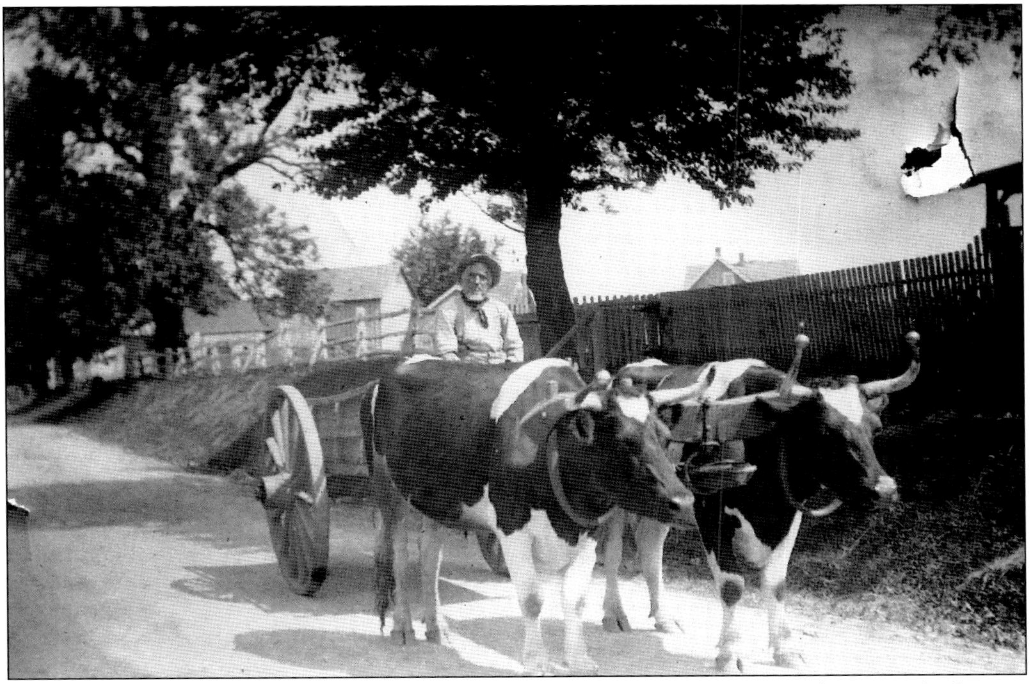

A man carries coal in an ox-driven wagon down Route 252 to Battles Greenhouses, which were located on what is now Delaware County Community College. (Hilda Lucas.)

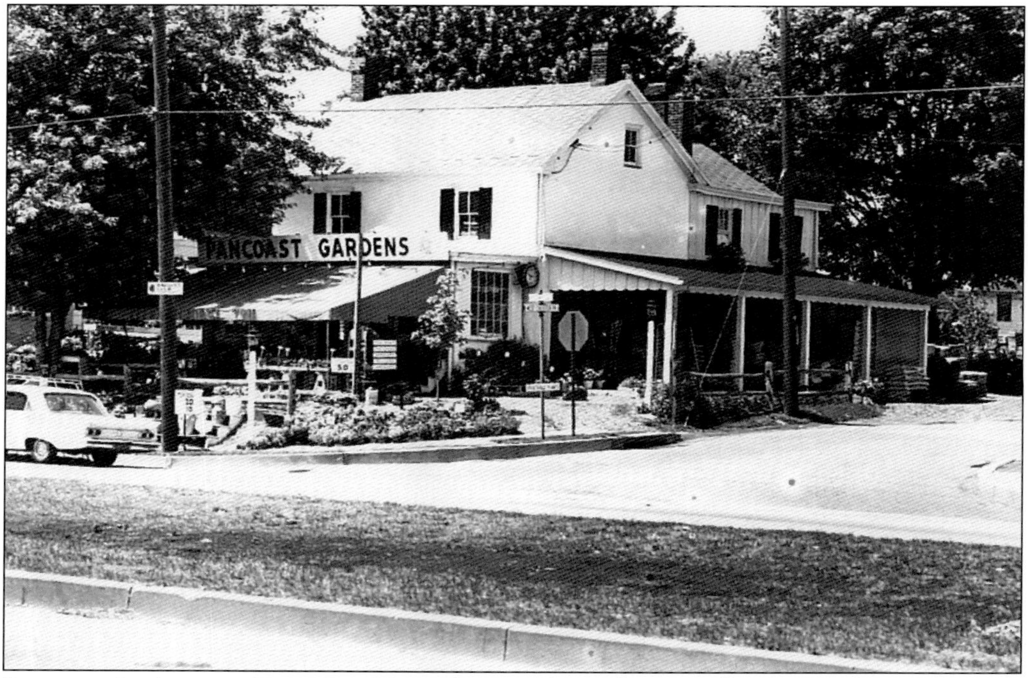

Pancoast Gardens was located at West Chester Pike and Broomall Avenue. This picture was taken in 1965. (Seth Pancoast.)

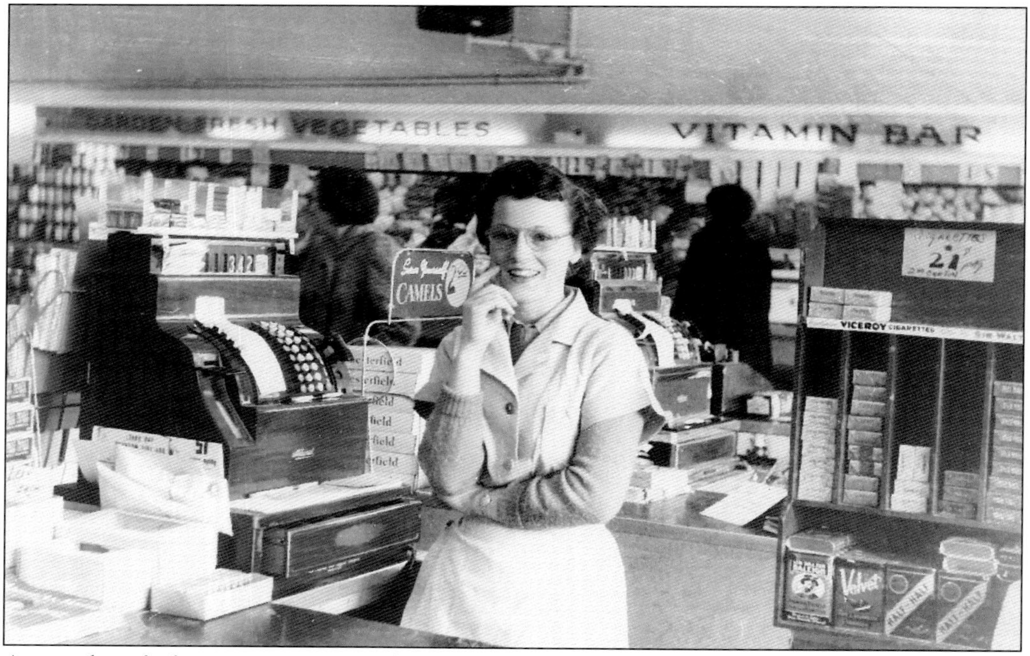

An unidentified woman mans a cash register at the old Acme store on West Chester Pike in Marple. (Al Vandetty.)

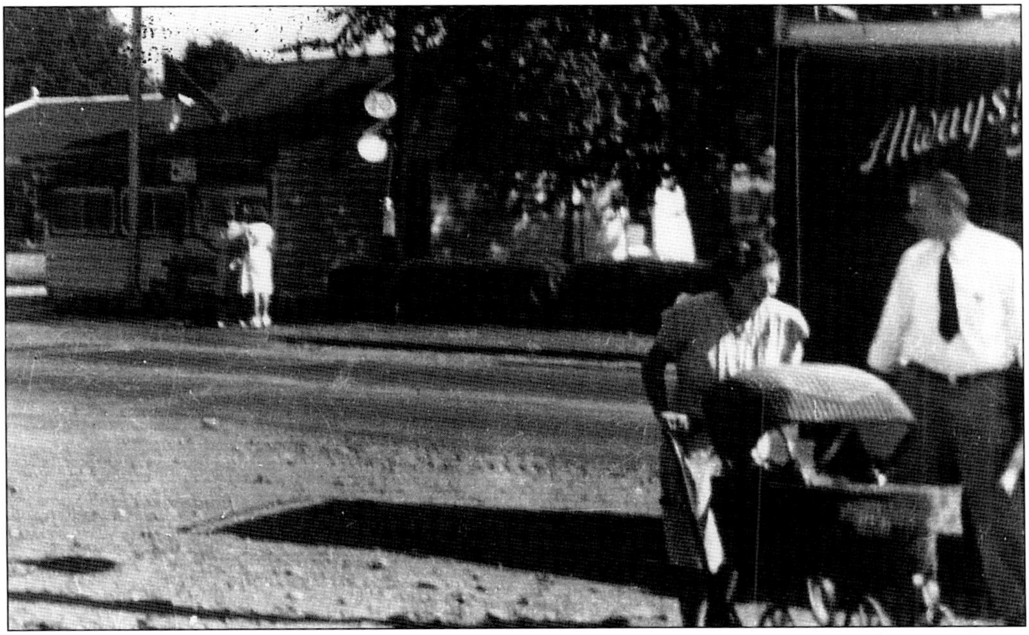

This image, taken in the early 1940s, shows Max Moyse's barbershop on West Chester Pike in Marple. (Seth Pancoast.)

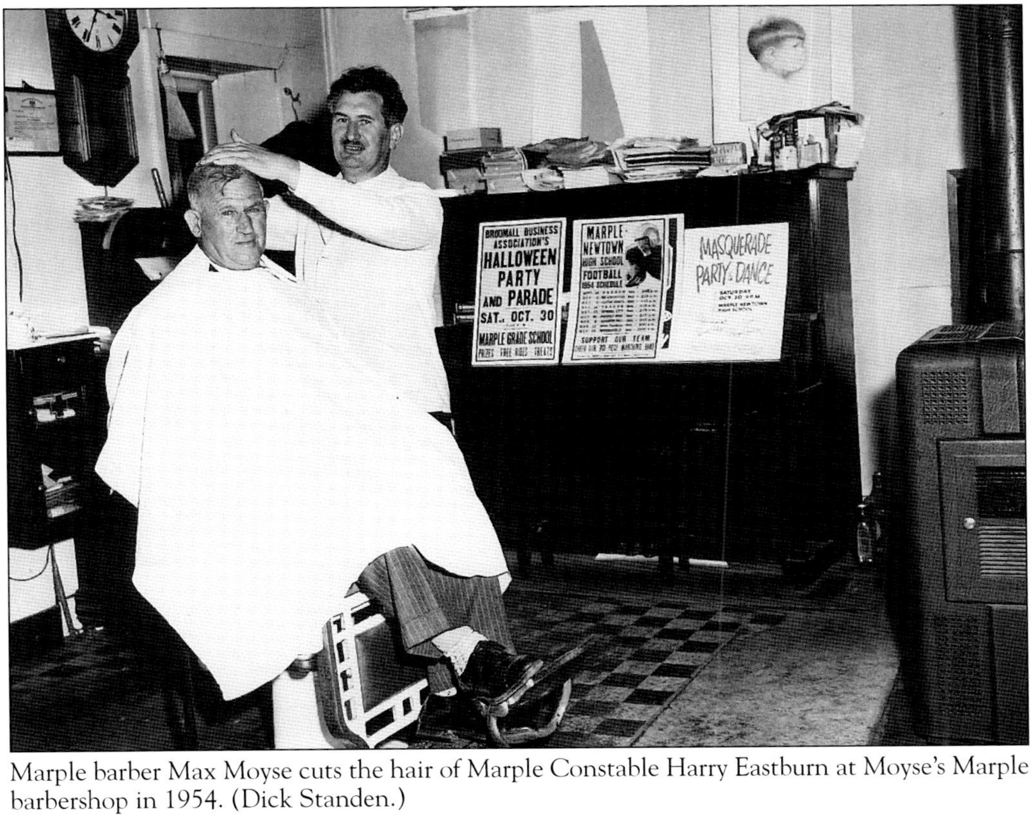

Marple barber Max Moyse cuts the hair of Marple Constable Harry Eastburn at Moyse's Marple barbershop in 1954. (Dick Standen.)

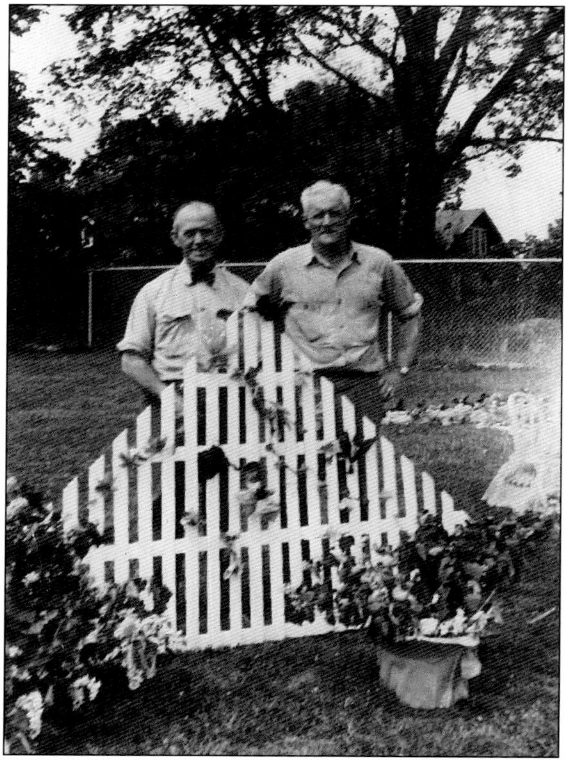

John McKinley and Charlie Thompson were two of Marple Township's first school bus drivers. (Dick Standen.)

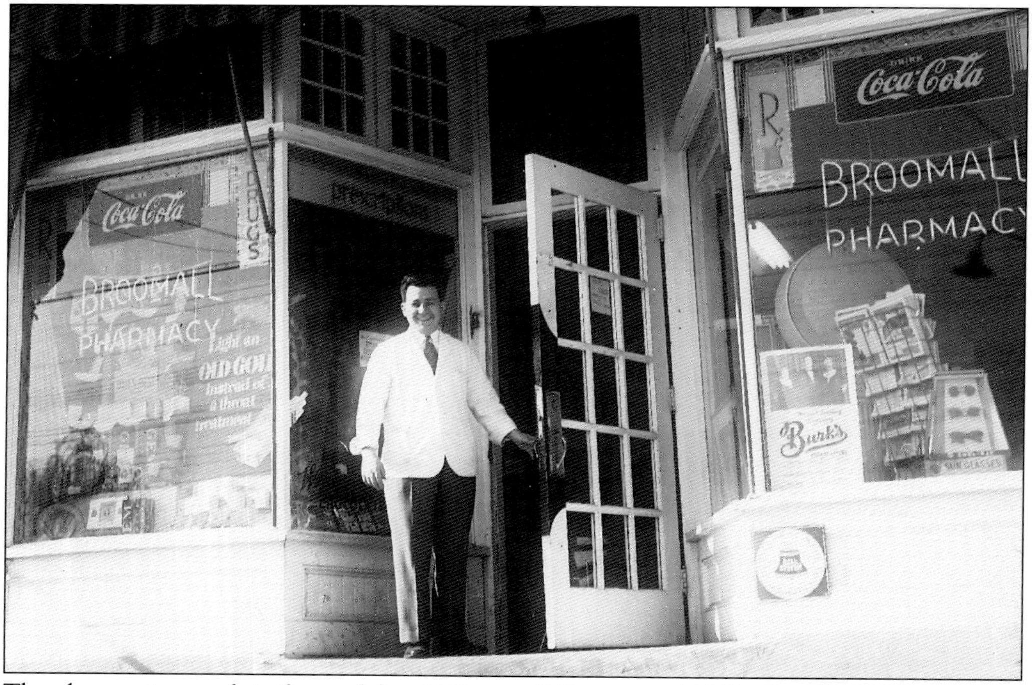

The pharmacist stands in front of the old Broomall Pharmacy. (Al Vandetty.)

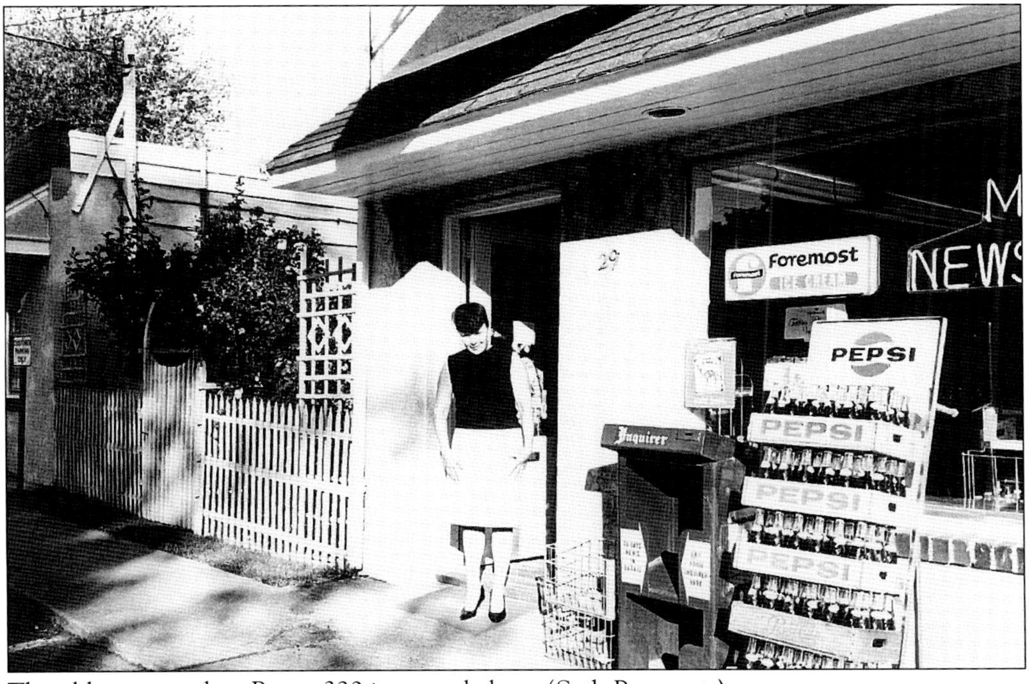

The old newsstand on Route 320 is now a bakery. (Seth Pancoast.)

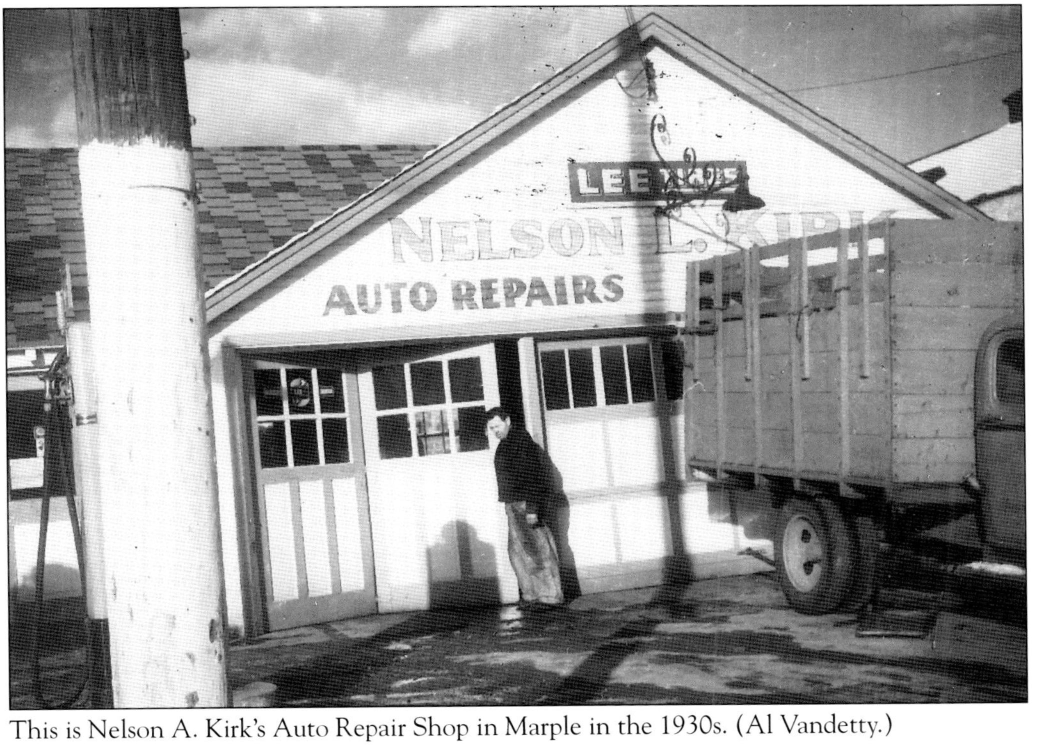

This is Nelson A. Kirk's Auto Repair Shop in Marple in the 1930s. (Al Vandetty.)

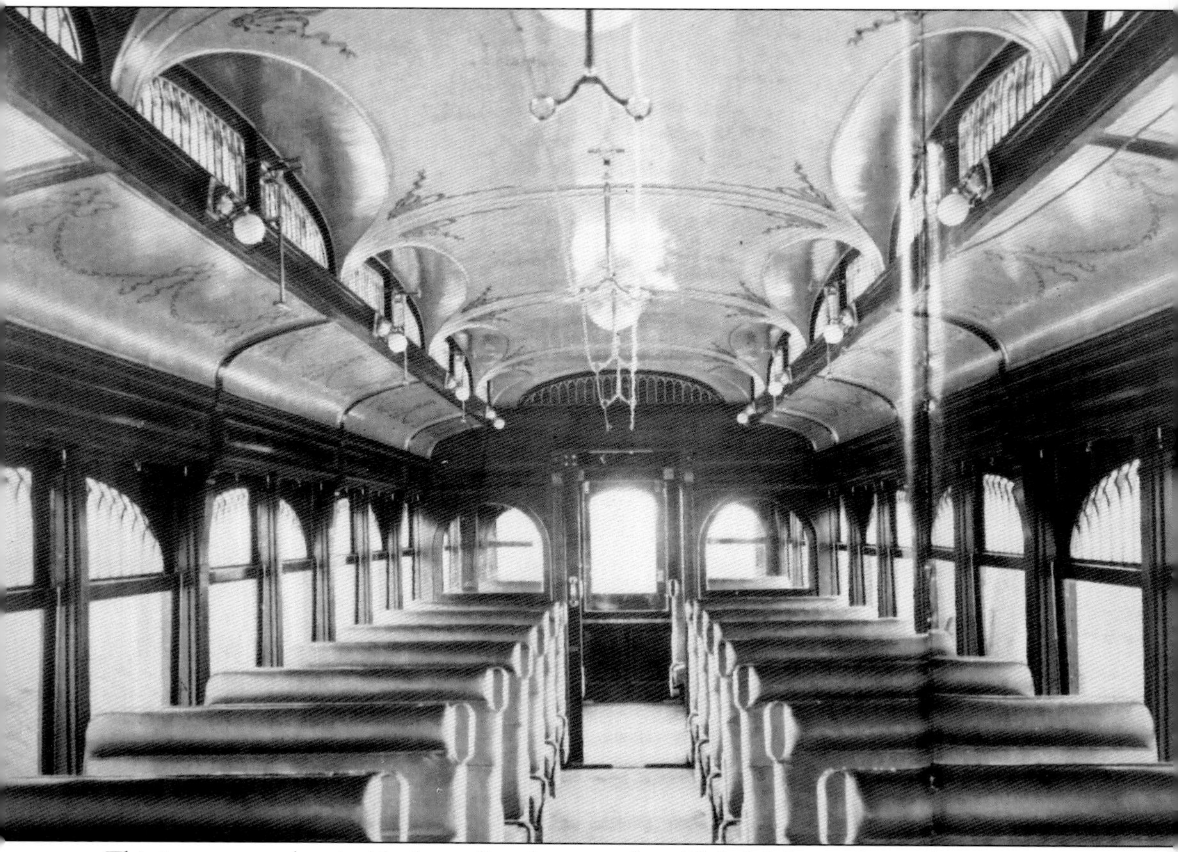

This image was taken inside the trolley that went from Philadelphia to West Chester. In addition to shuttling supplies from Philadelphia to the outlying rural areas, the trolley transported passengers to amusement parks such as Castle Rock in Edgmont and Broomall Grove in Marple. (Hilda Lucas.)

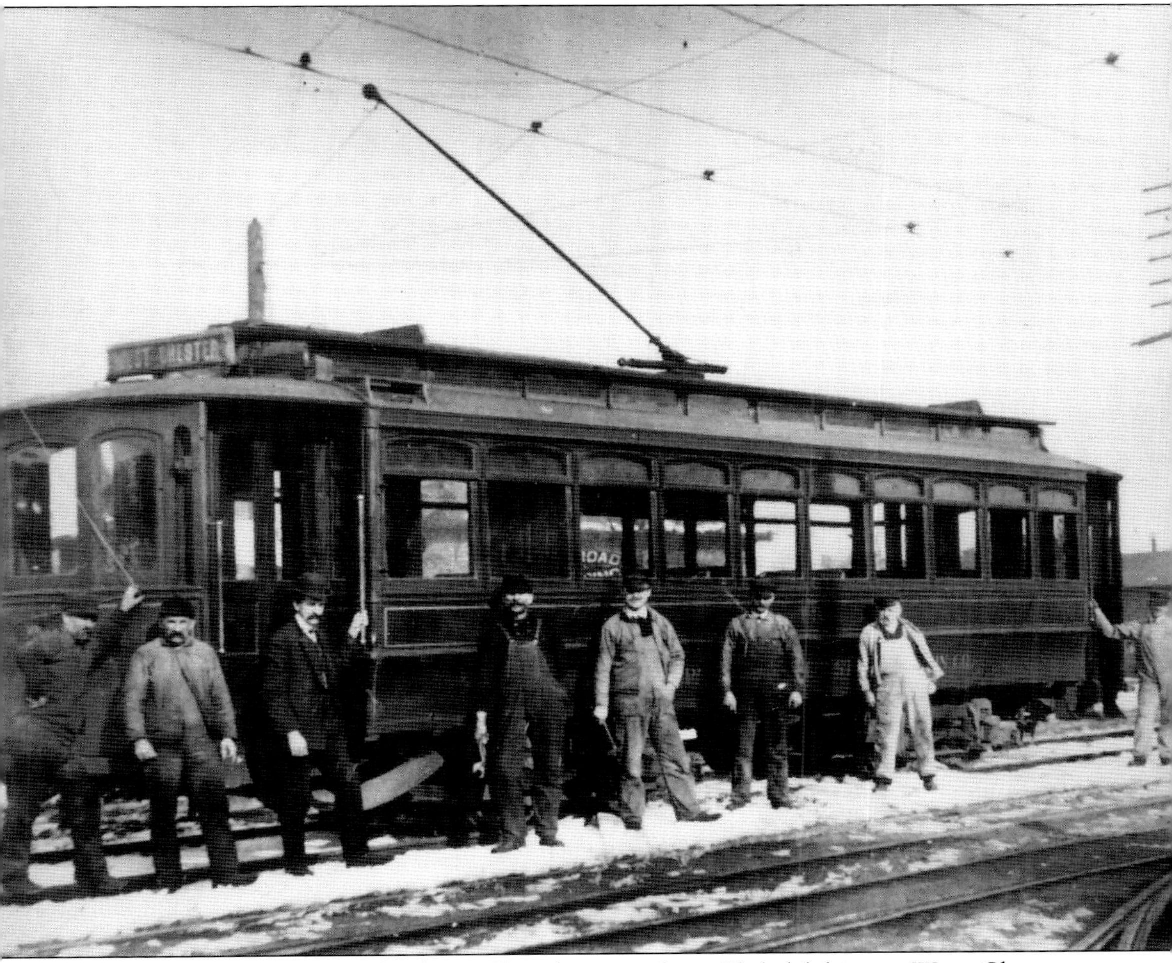

Railroad workers pose outside the trolley that ran from Philadelphia to West Chester. (Hilda Lucas.)

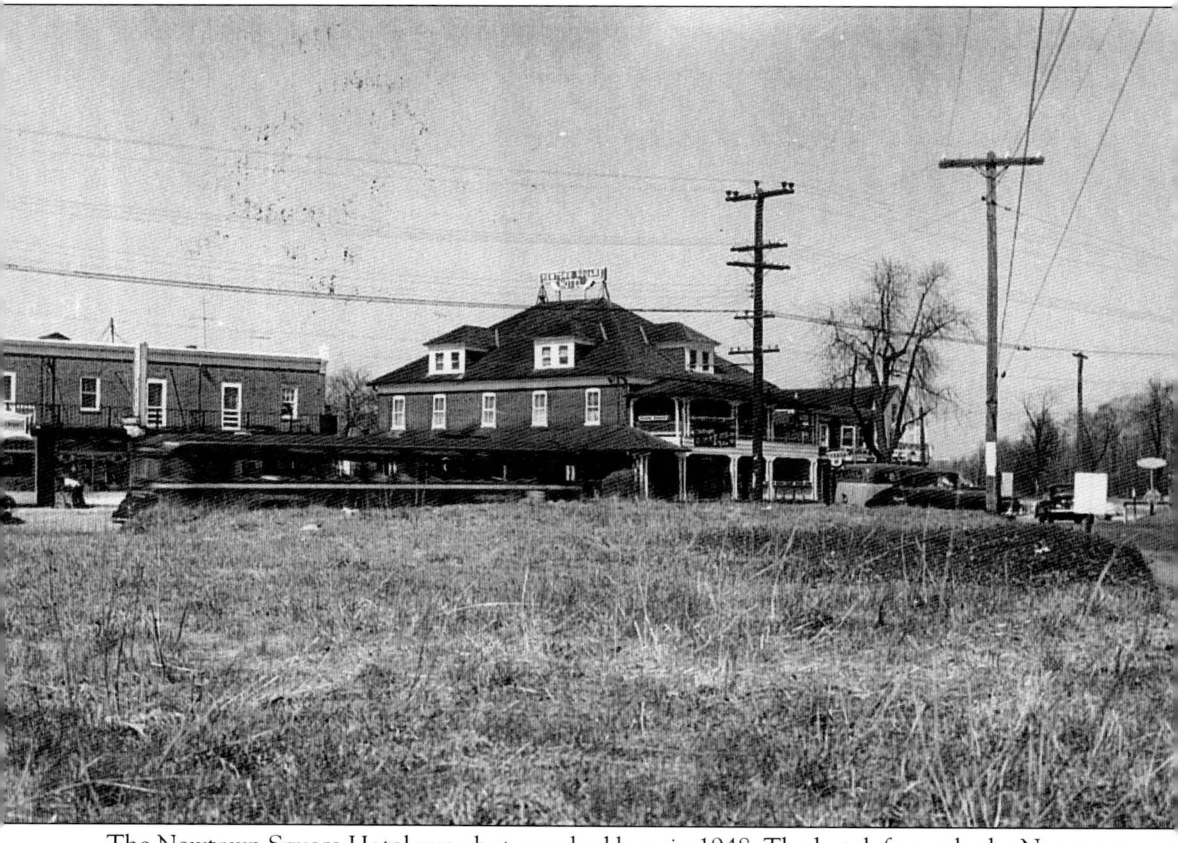

The Newtown Square Hotel was photographed here in 1948. The hotel, formerly the Newtown Square Inn, was the social center of Newtown Township for many years before it was demolished in 1969. (Seth Pancoast.)

Three

Country Crossroads

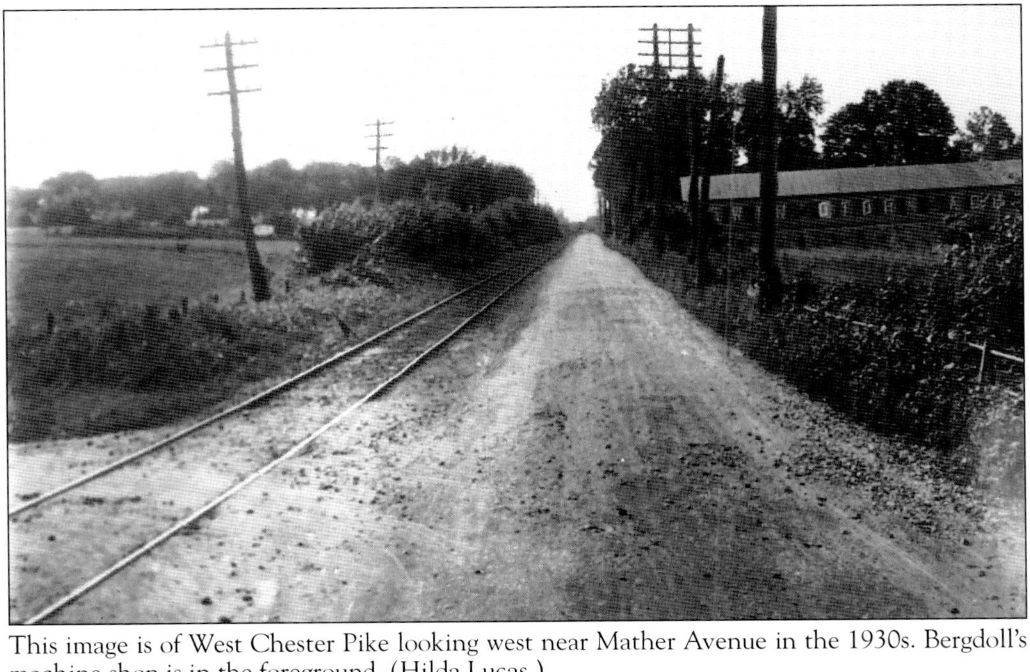

This image is of West Chester Pike looking west near Mather Avenue in the 1930s. Bergdoll's machine shop is in the foreground. (Hilda Lucas.)

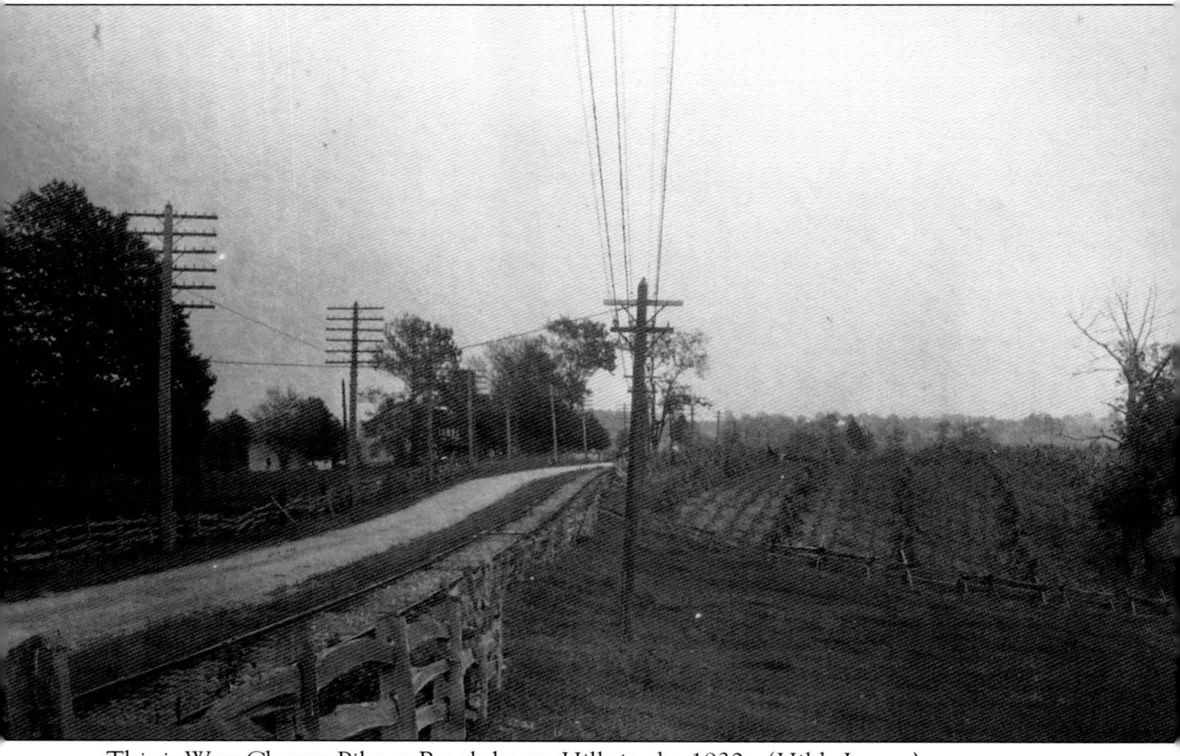

This is West Chester Pike at Brookthorpe Hills in the 1930s. (Hilda Lucas.)

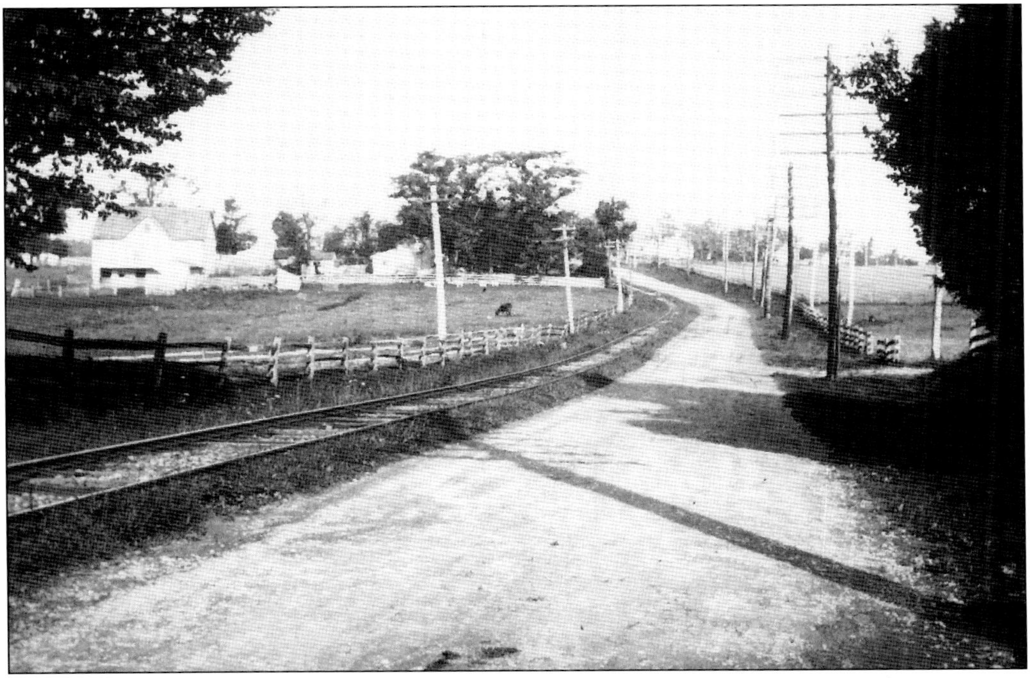

The Hanley Farm was located on West Chester Pike on the site of the present-day Newtown Square Shopping Center. (Hilda Lucas.)

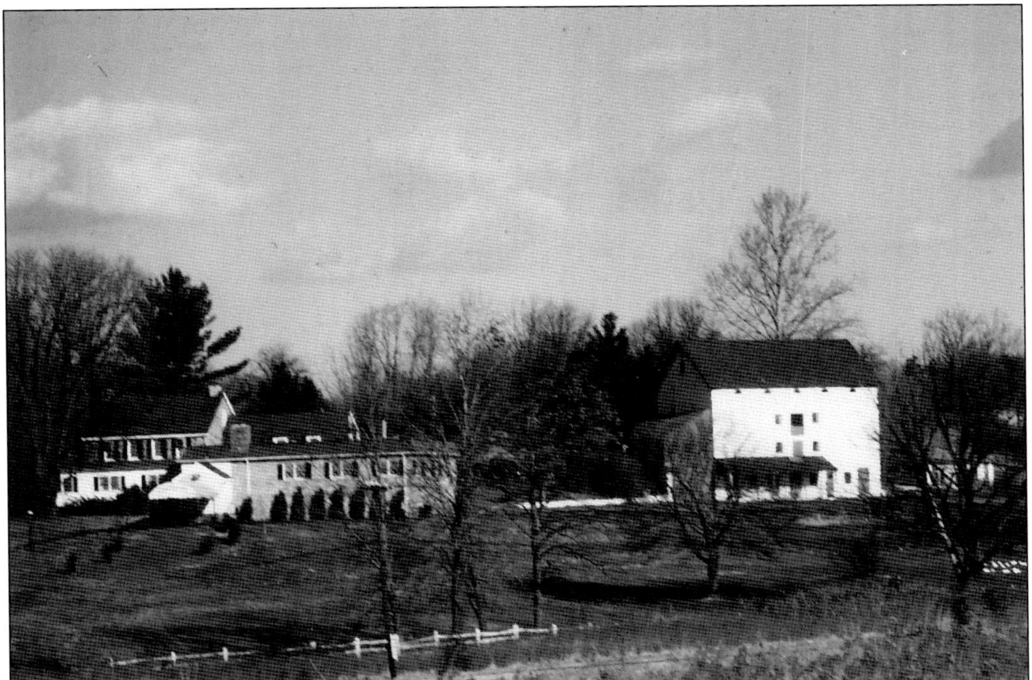

The Newtown Squire and the adjacent barn are shown here about 1964. (Hilda Lucas.)

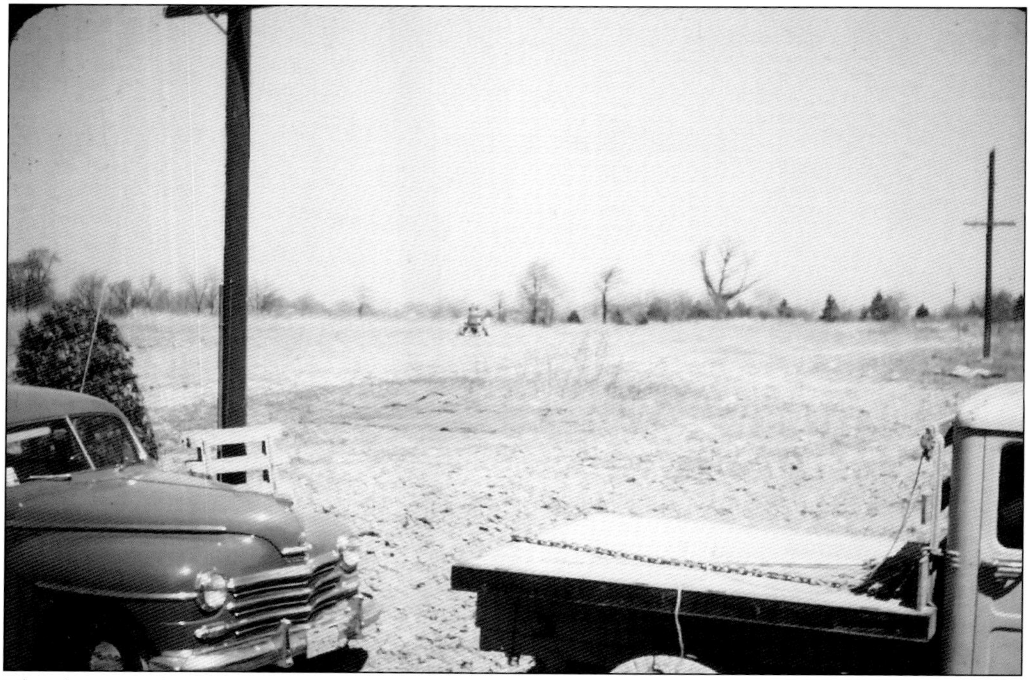

This farm was located on the site of Russell School. (Hilda Lucas.)

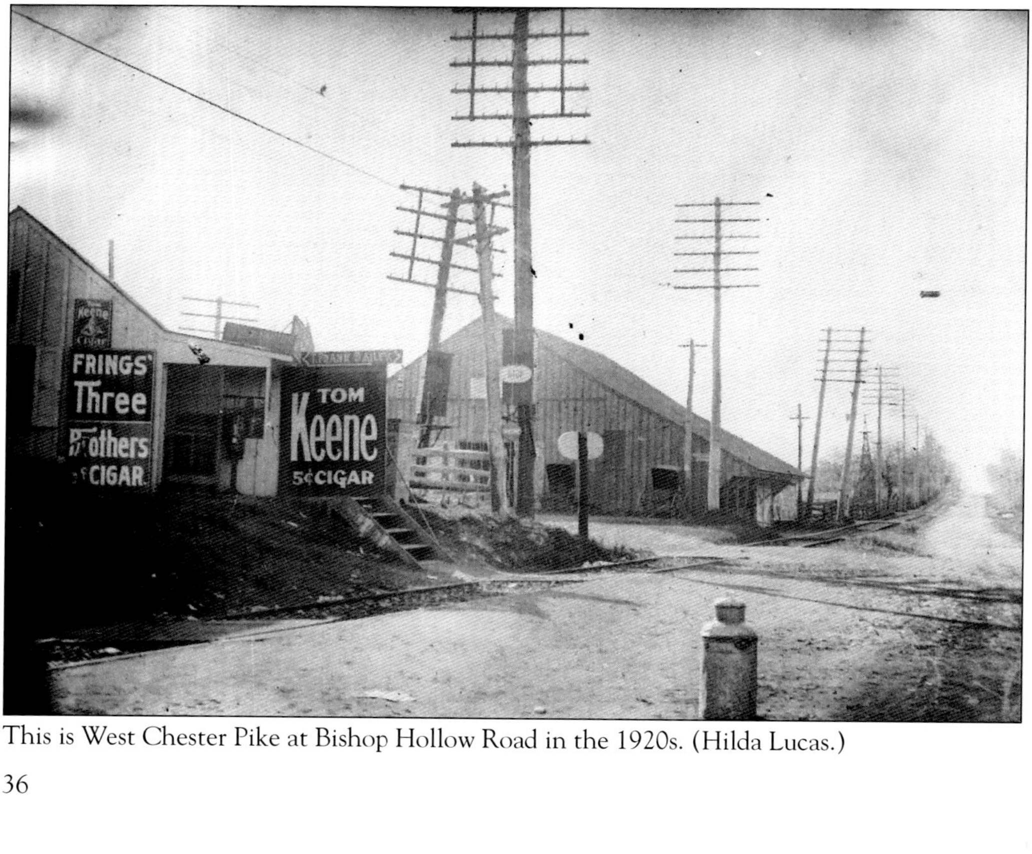

This is West Chester Pike at Bishop Hollow Road in the 1920s. (Hilda Lucas.)

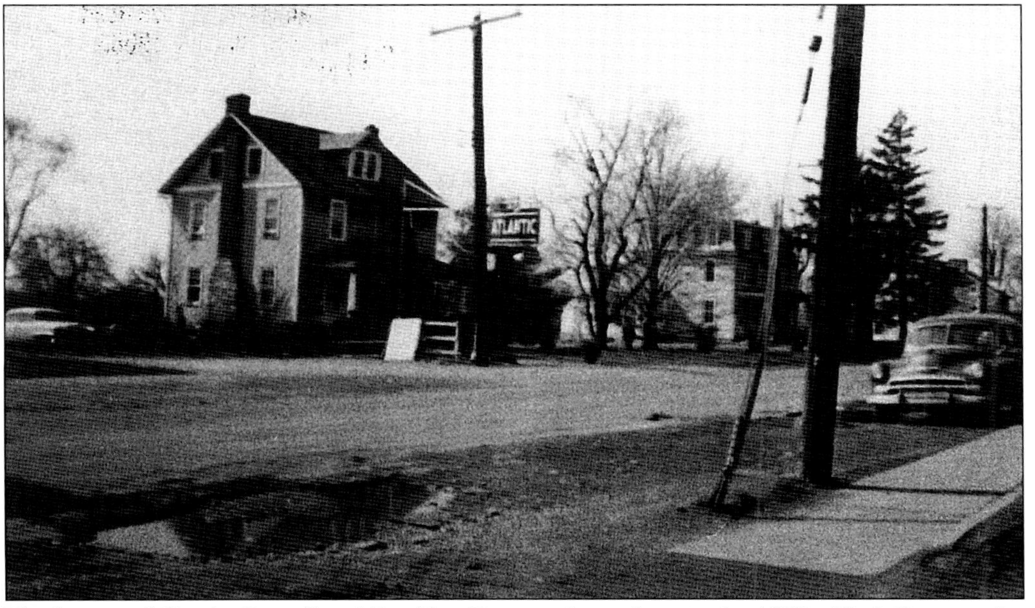

The homes of Charles Russell and Franklin Getz are shown here in the 1930s. (Seth Pancoast.)

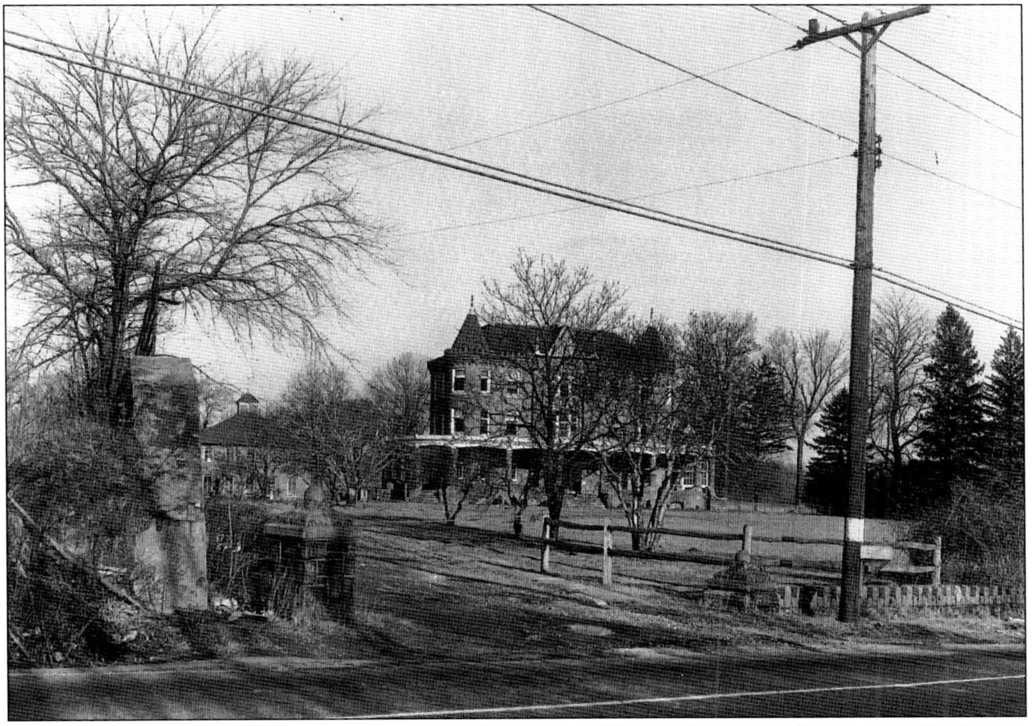

The Bergdoll Mansion stood on the west side of West Chester Pike near Interstate 476. It was built by the Bergdoll family around the turn of the century and was home to Grover Cleveland Bergdoll, the most infamous draft dodger of World War I. The mansion burned down in the mid-1970s. (John Kuseian.)

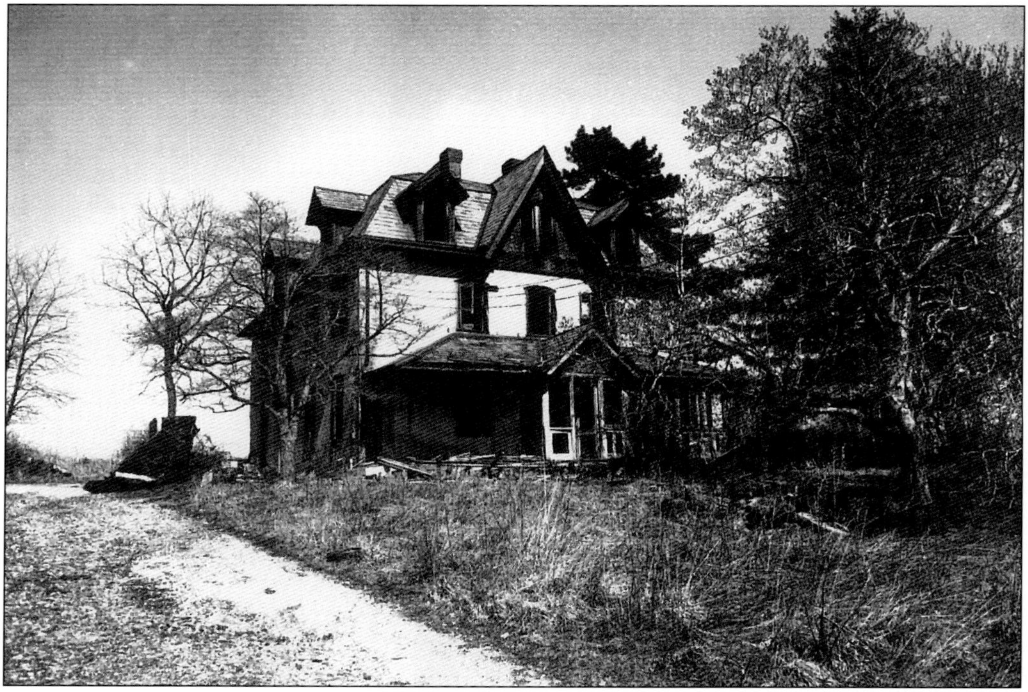

This old house was located on the Bergdoll property. (Seth Pancoast.)

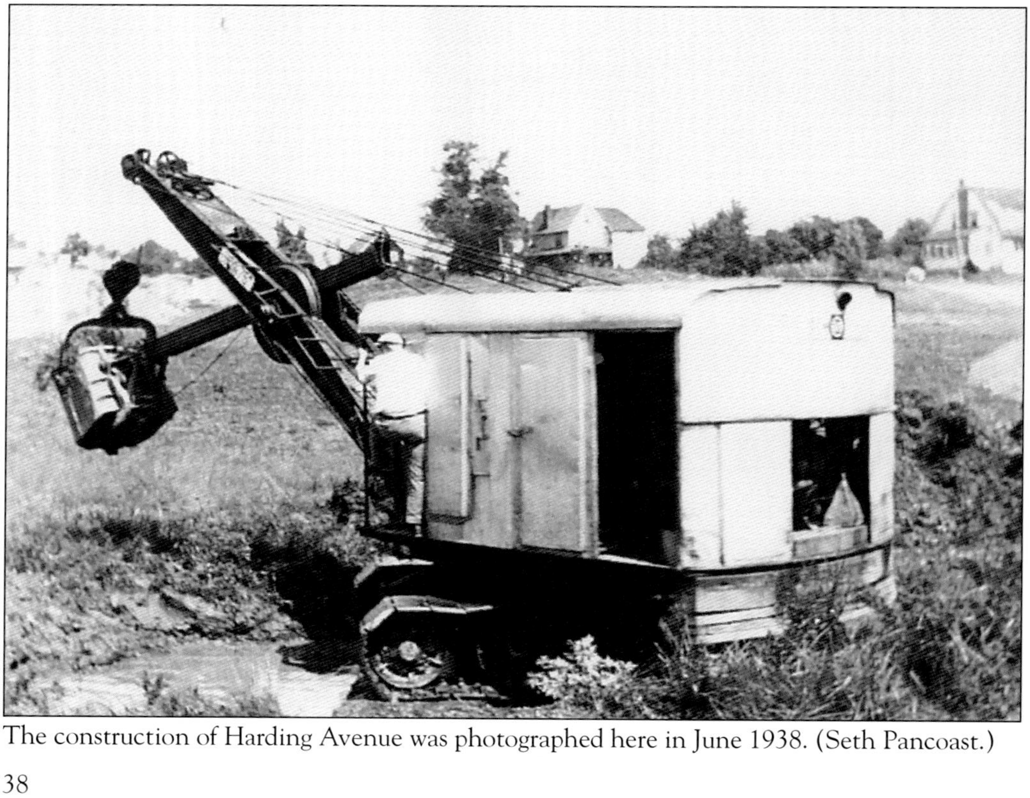

The construction of Harding Avenue was photographed here in June 1938. (Seth Pancoast.)

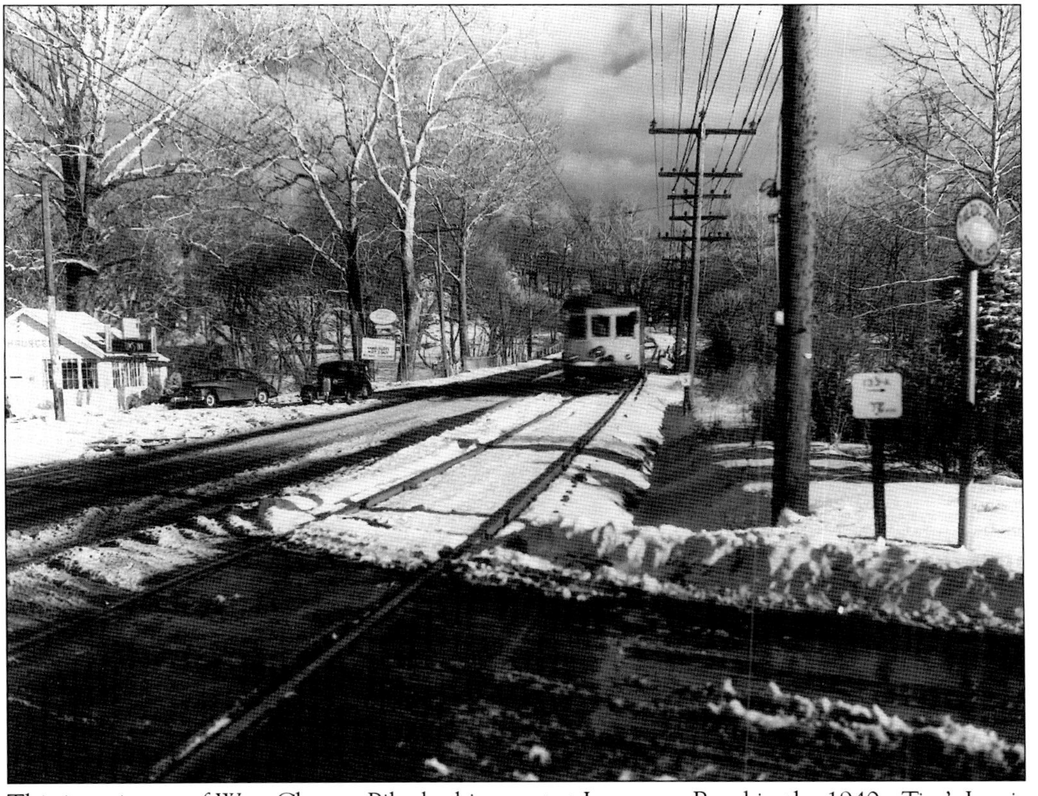

This is an image of West Chester Pike looking east at Lawrence Road in the 1940s. Tim's Inn is in the foreground. (Bill Greco.)

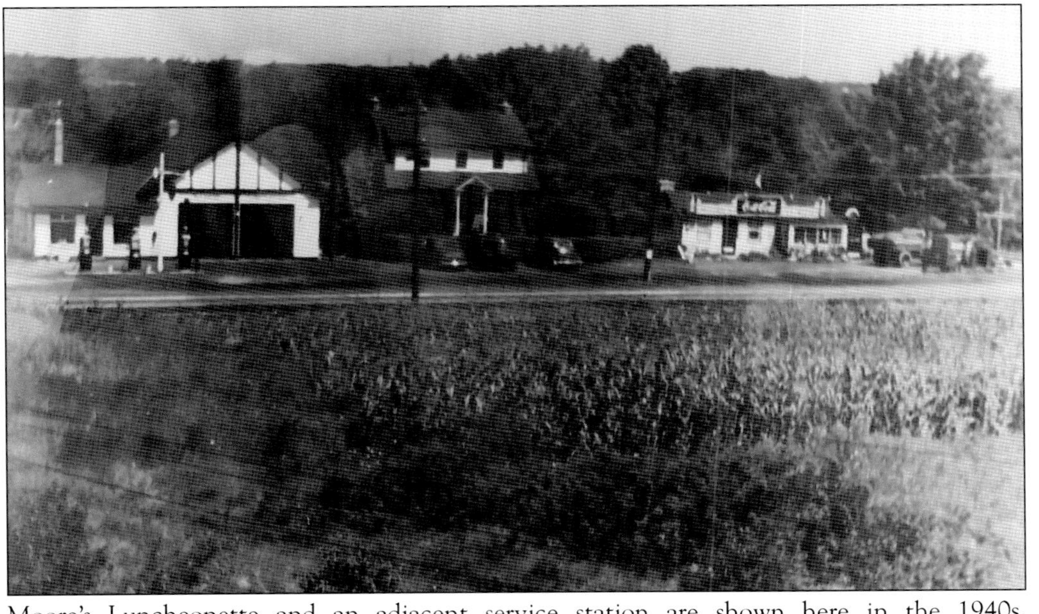

Moore's Luncheonette and an adjacent service station are shown here in the 1940s. (Al Vandetty.)

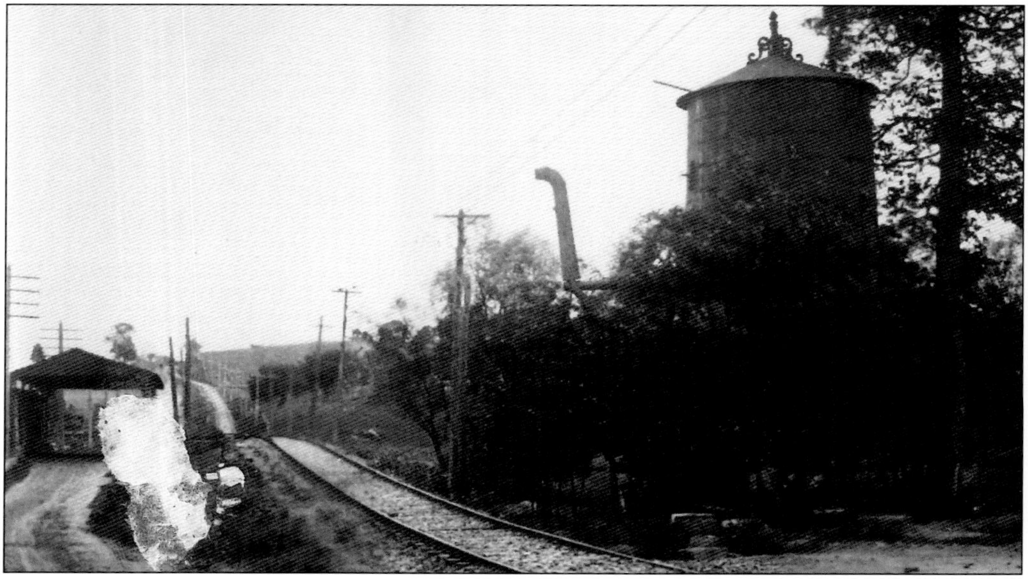

This covered bridge and adjacent water tower were located along West Chester Pike near Castle Rock. (Hilda Lucas.)

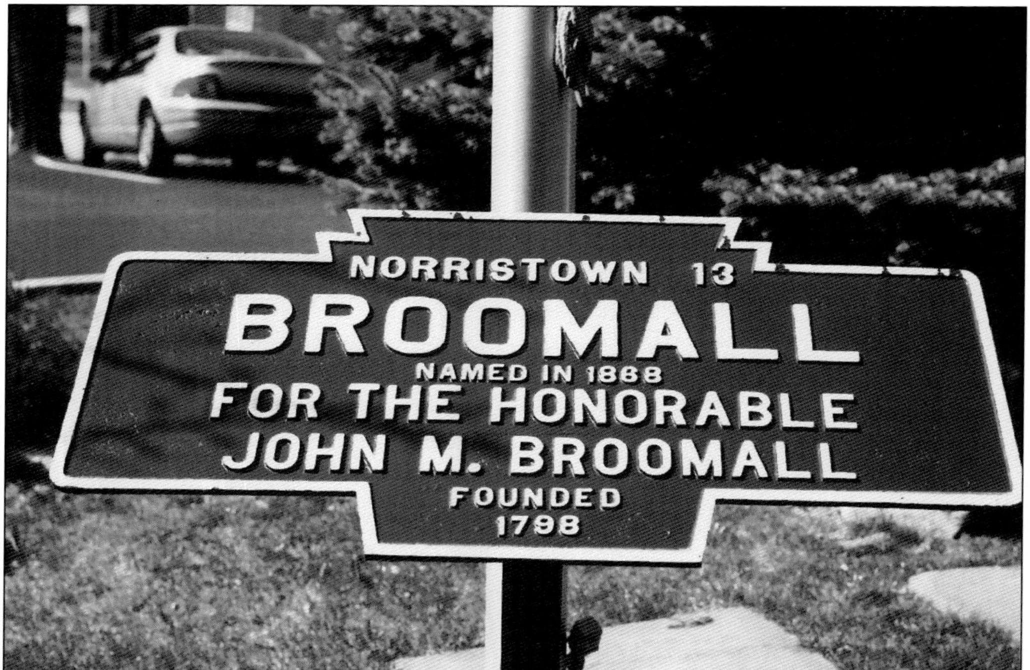

Four of these Broomall signs were erected at various points in Marple Township. This one stands in front of the Marple Township Municipal Building. (Mike Mathis.)

Four

COMMUNITY FOUNDATIONS

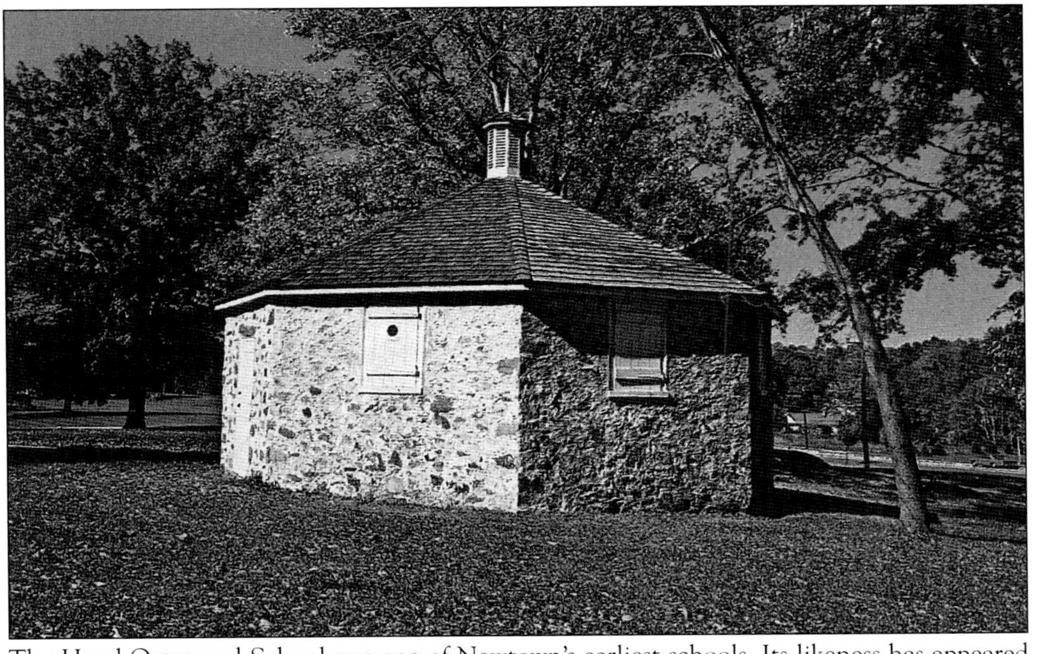

The Hood Octagonal School was one of Newtown's earliest schools. Its likeness has appeared on Marple Newtown High School rings. (Richard Plotts.)

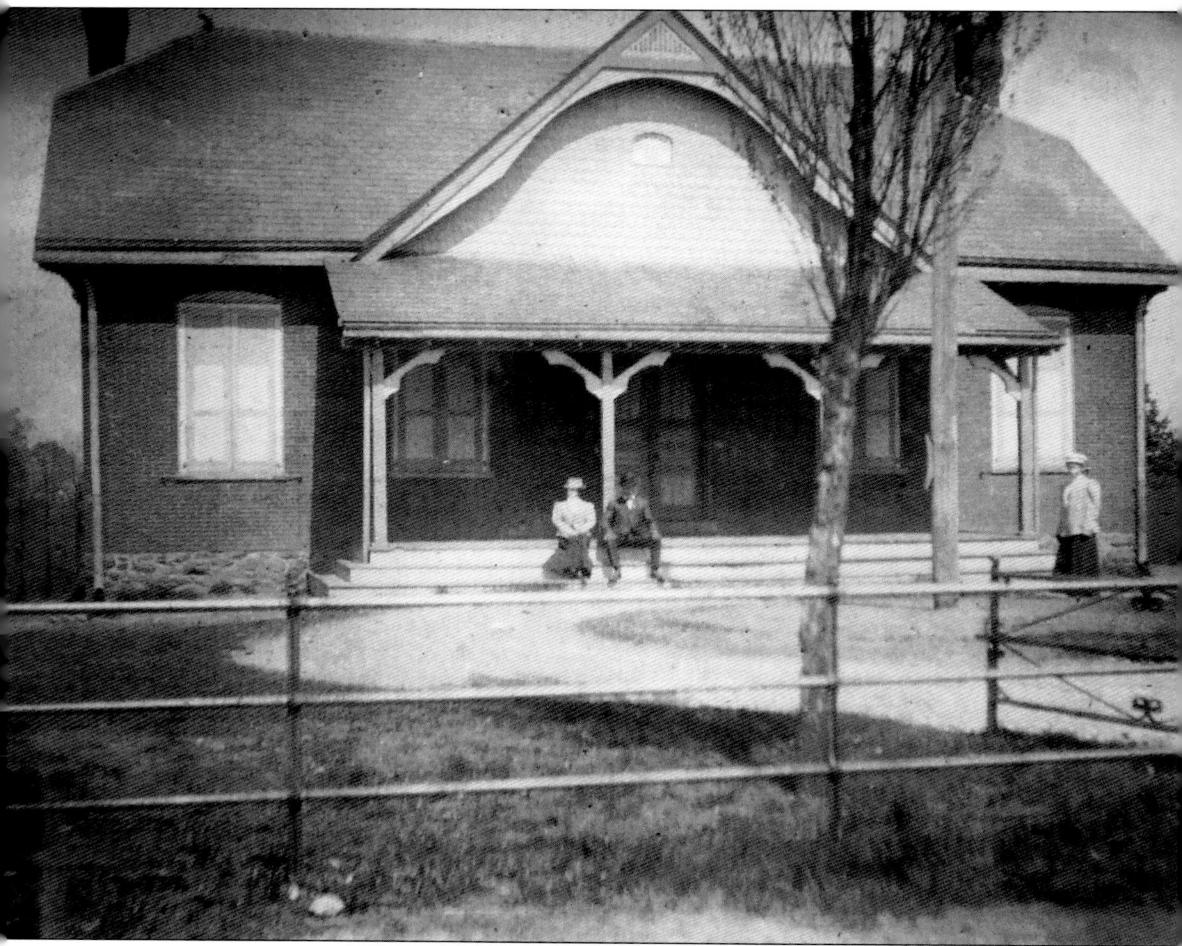

This early Newtown Township school stood at Route 252 and Mary Jane Lane. (Hilda Lucas.)

This image was taken during the laying of the cornerstone for the Marple School in 1922. (Hilda Lucas.)

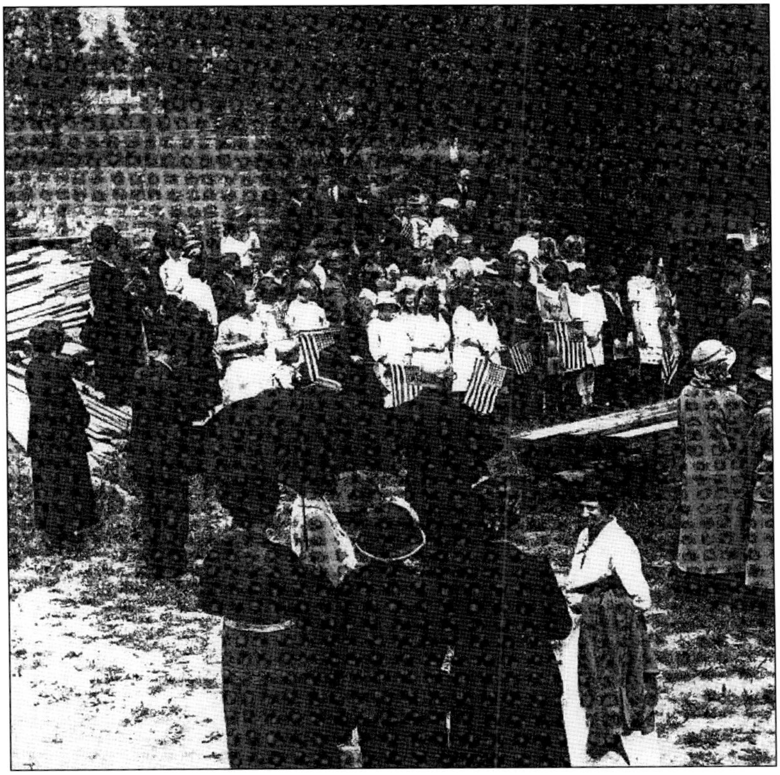

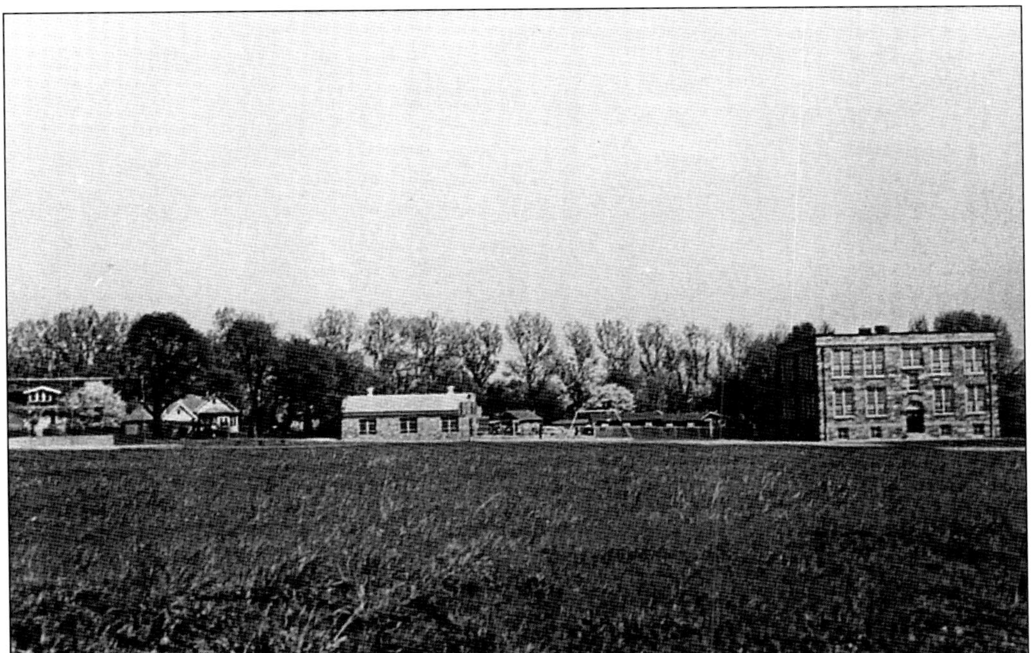

This is an image of the Marple School and adjacent fields. (Seth Pancoast.)

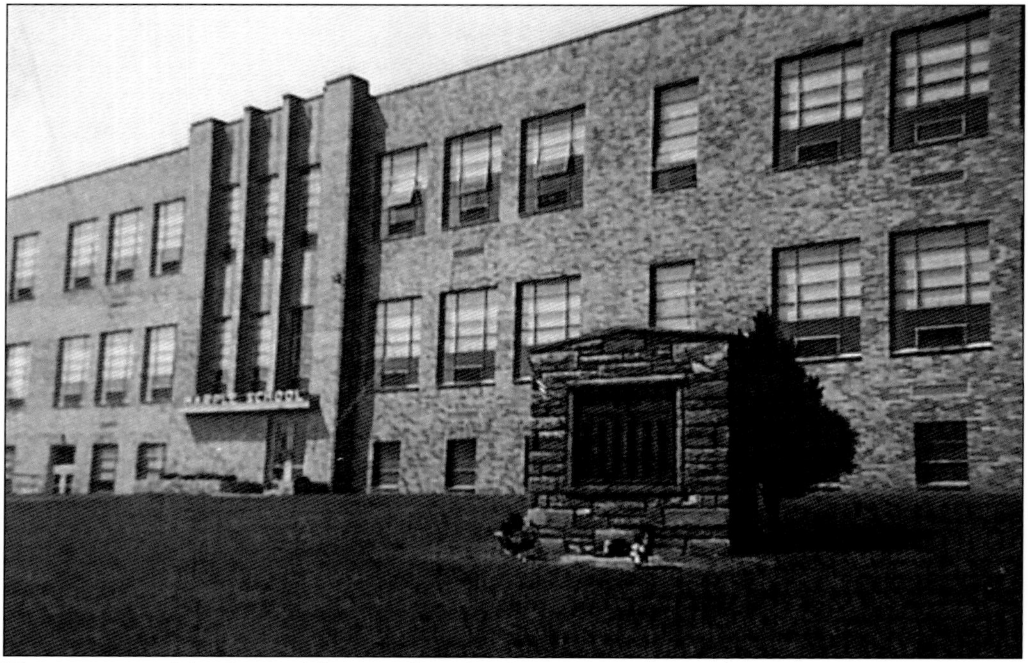

This image is of the front of the Marple School with the veteran's monument, which has since been moved to the American Legion hall on West Chester Pike. (Jan Ceton.)

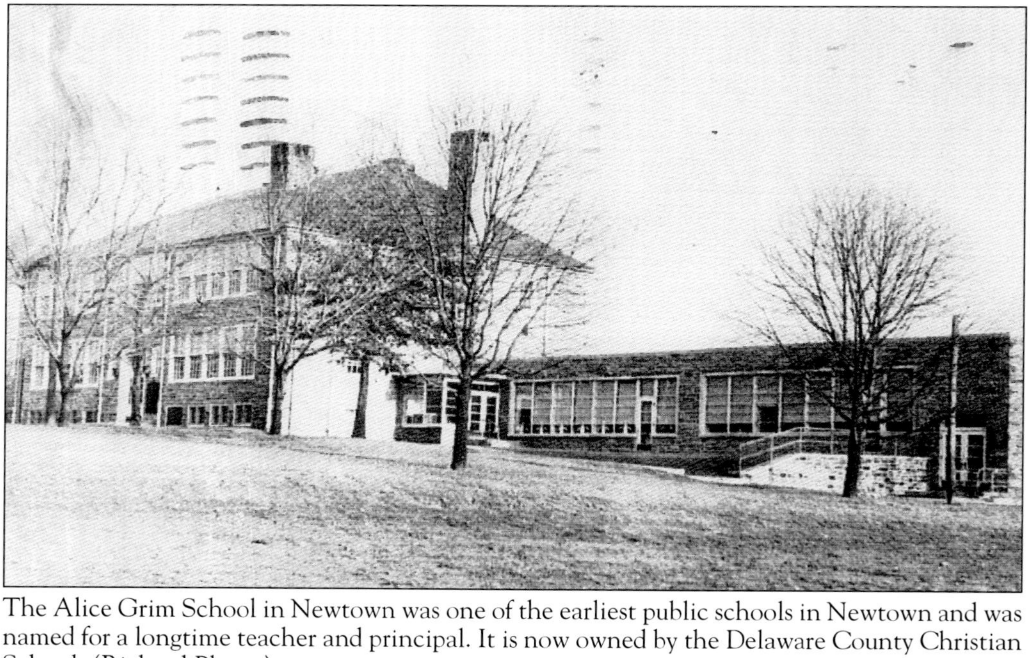

The Alice Grim School in Newtown was one of the earliest public schools in Newtown and was named for a longtime teacher and principal. It is now owned by the Delaware County Christian School. (Richard Plotts.)

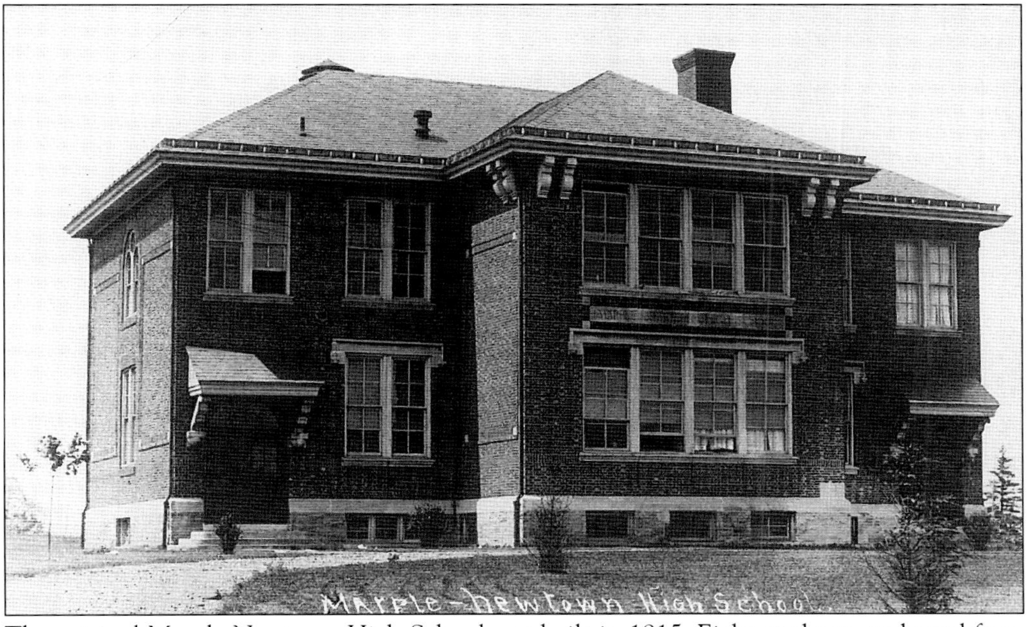

The original Marple Newtown High School was built in 1915. Eight students graduated from the school's first class in 1916. (Richard Plotts.)

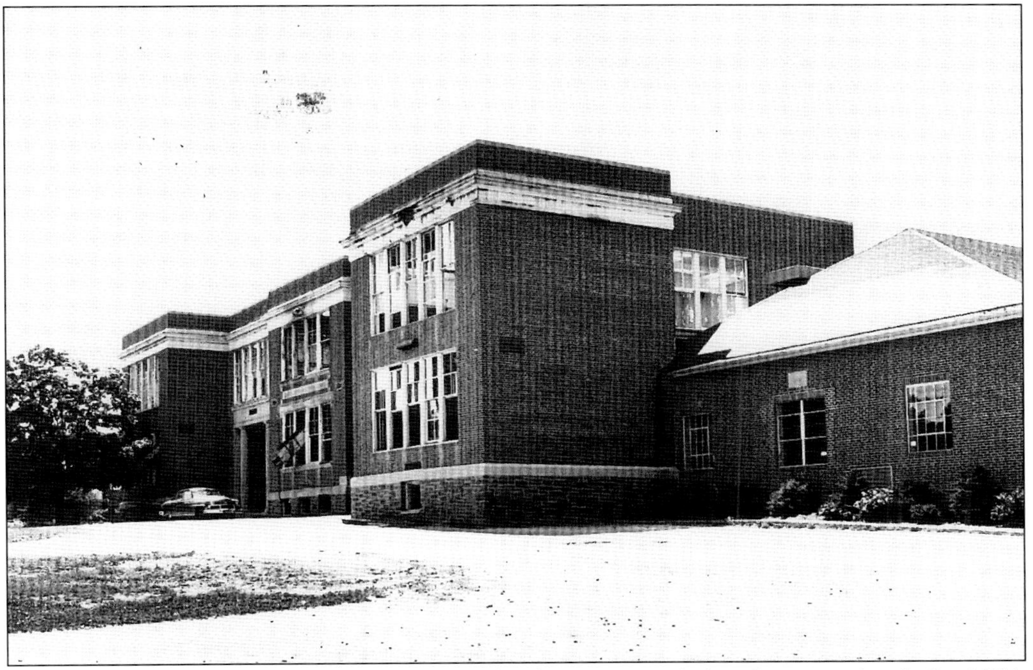
The original Marple Newtown High School was gutted by fire on April 9, 1956. (Seth Pancoast.)

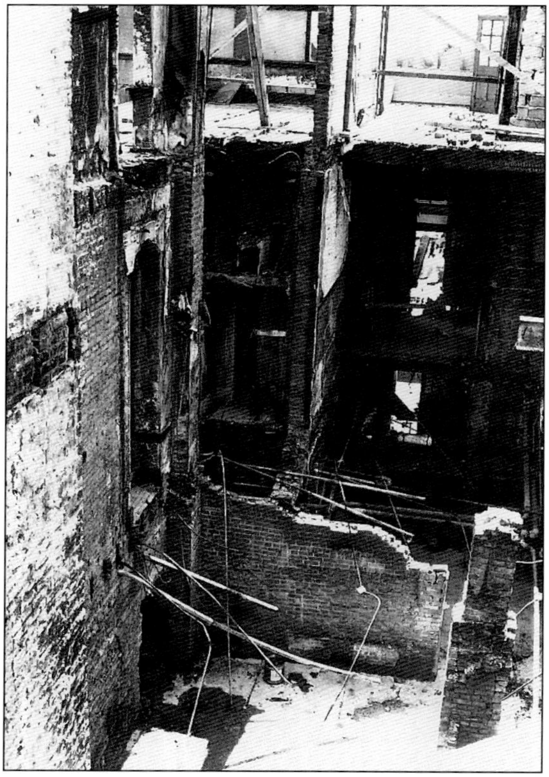

This image was taken looking through the floorboards of the fire-ravaged Marple Newtown High School. (Seth Pancoast.)

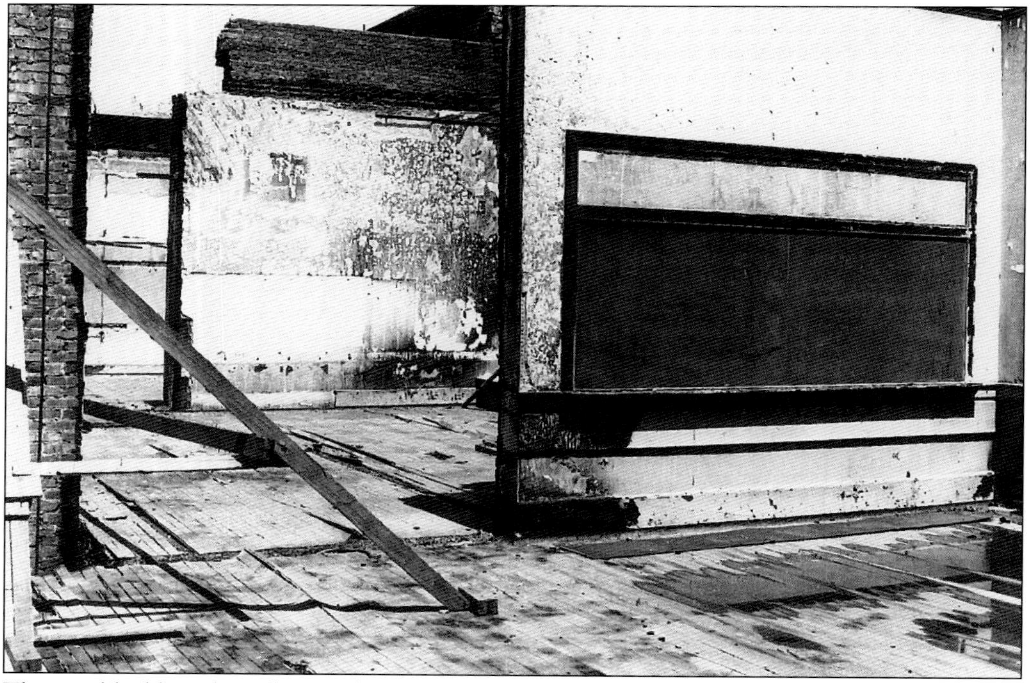

This is a blackboard inside Marple Newtown High School after the fire. (Seth Pancoast.)

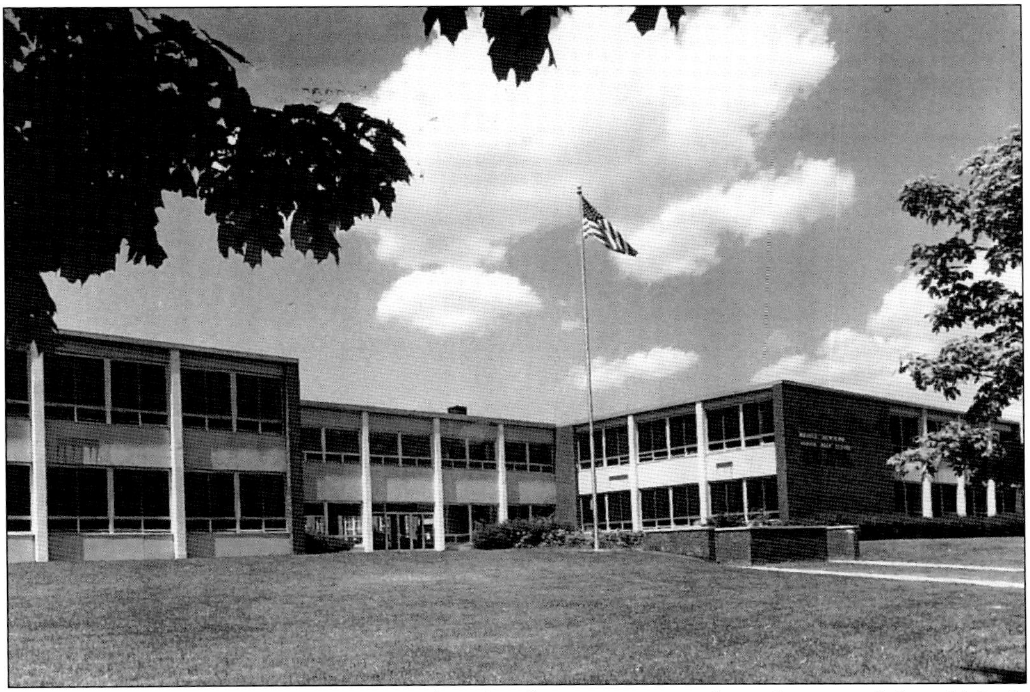

The new Marple Newtown Junior High School was constructed on the site of the old high school after the April 1956 fire. The school, along with Paxon Hollow Junior High School, housed students in grades six through nine. It closed in the late 1970s. (Seth Pancoast.)

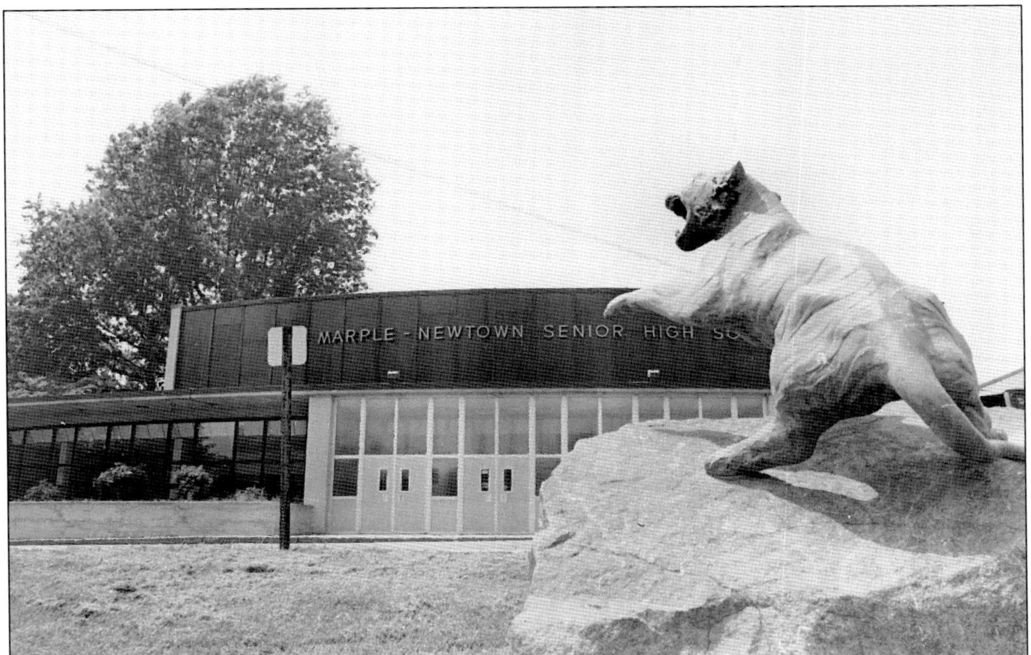

The present Marple Newtown High School was built after the 1956 fire devastated the original building. (Mike Perillo.)

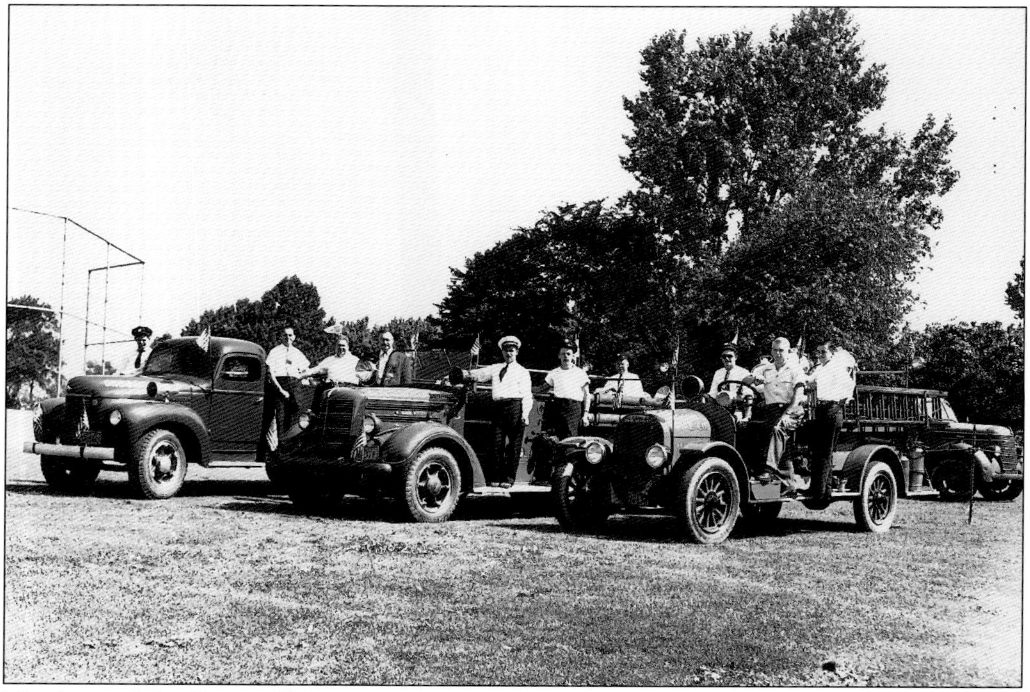

Members of the Broomall Fire Co. display the department's vehicles in this 1940s image. (Seth Pancoast.)

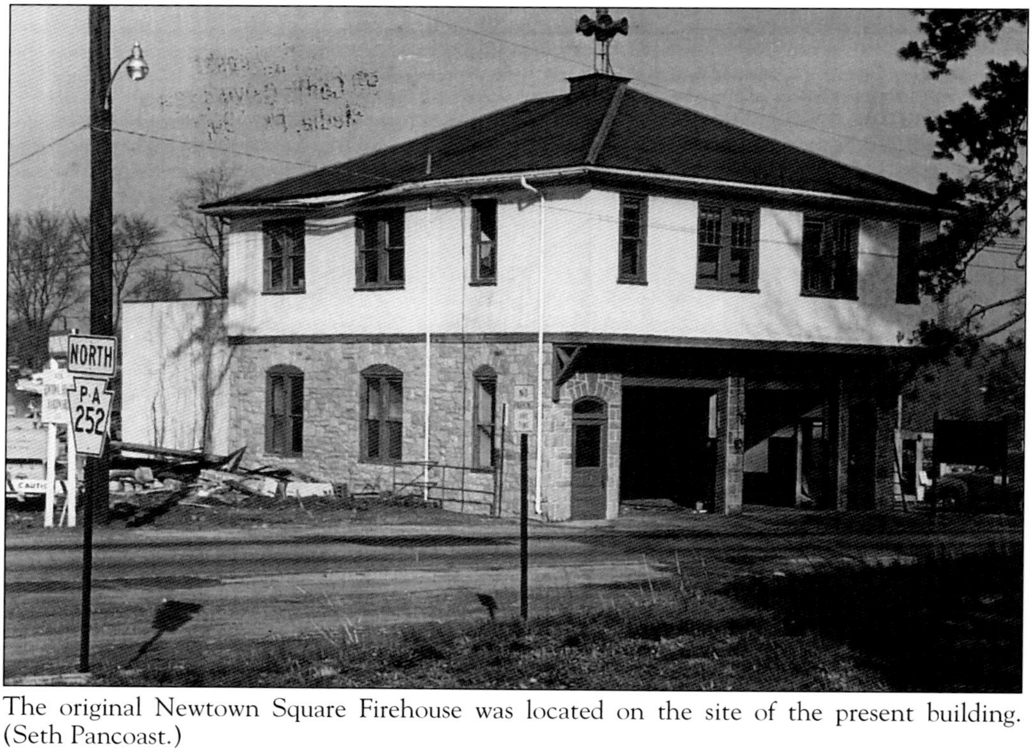

The original Newtown Square Firehouse was located on the site of the present building. (Seth Pancoast.)

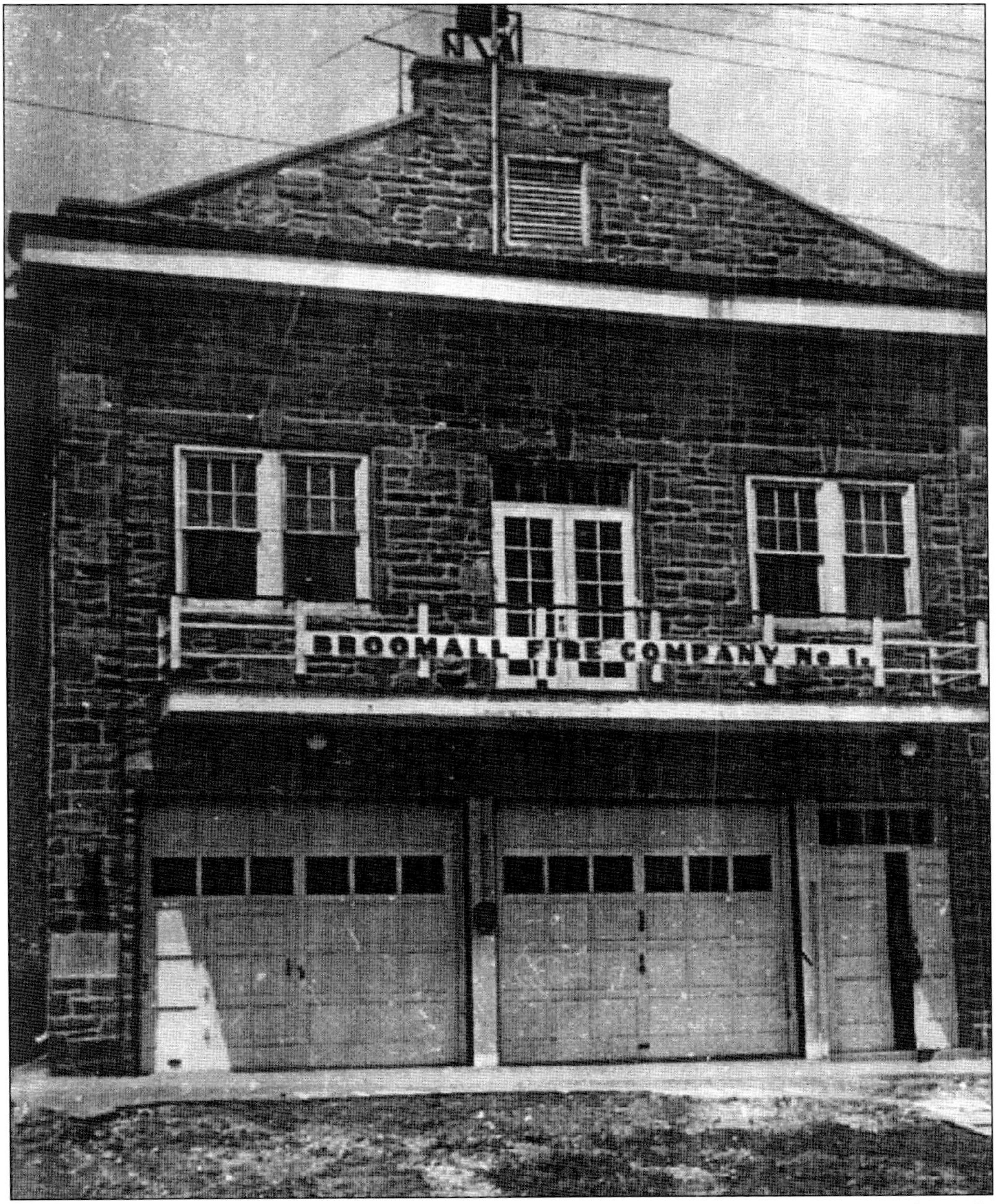

The original Broomall Firehouse was located on West Chester Pike near Route 320. (Marple Newtown Historical Society.)

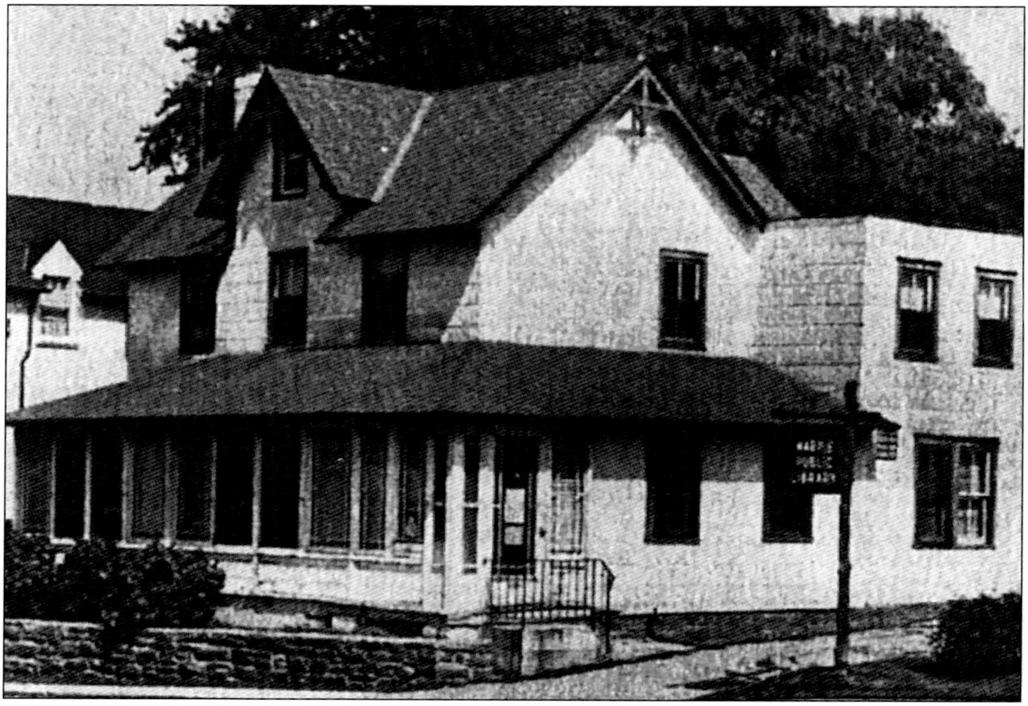

The original Marple Public Library was formerly Wilde's Tea Room. (Marple Newtown Historical Society.)

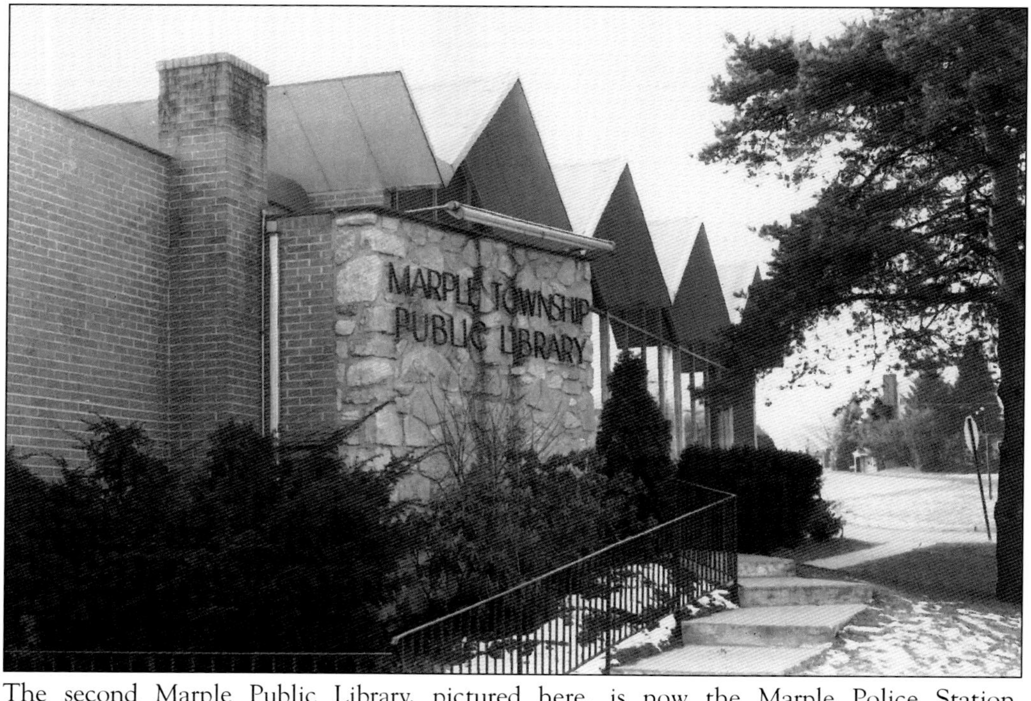

The second Marple Public Library, pictured here, is now the Marple Police Station. (*County Press.*)

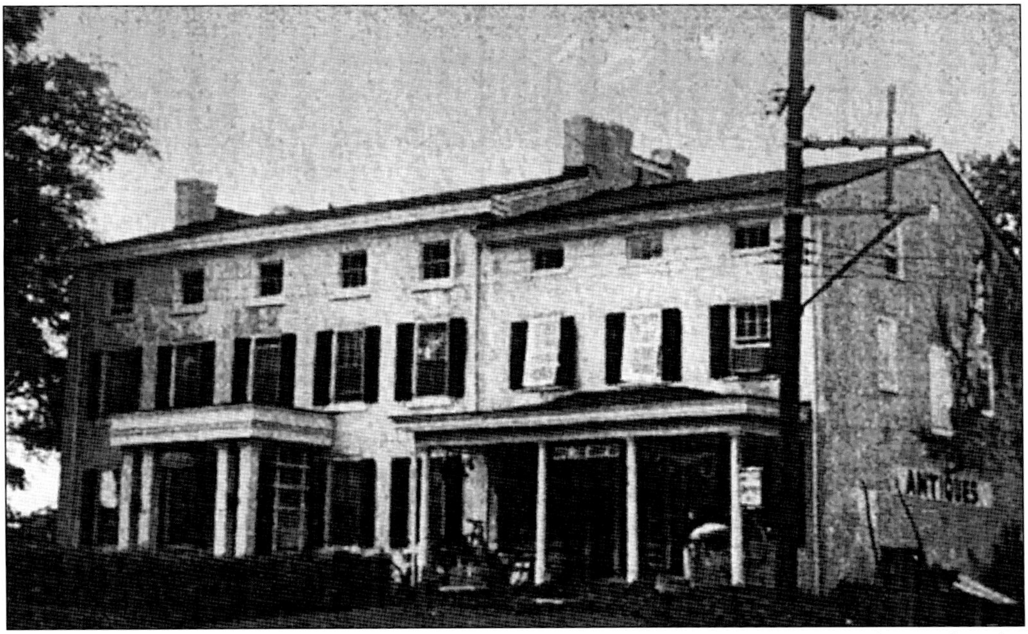

The Marple Post Office was located in the general store of Ebenezer R. Curtis and served as the post office for Marple Township from 1849 to 1903. (Marple Newtown Historical Society.)

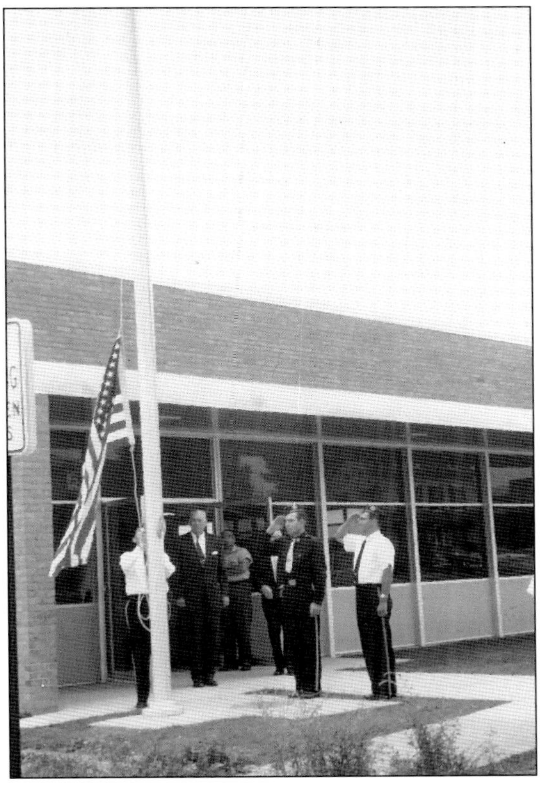

This image was taken at the dedication of the present Broomall Post Office in 1960. (Hilda Lucas.)

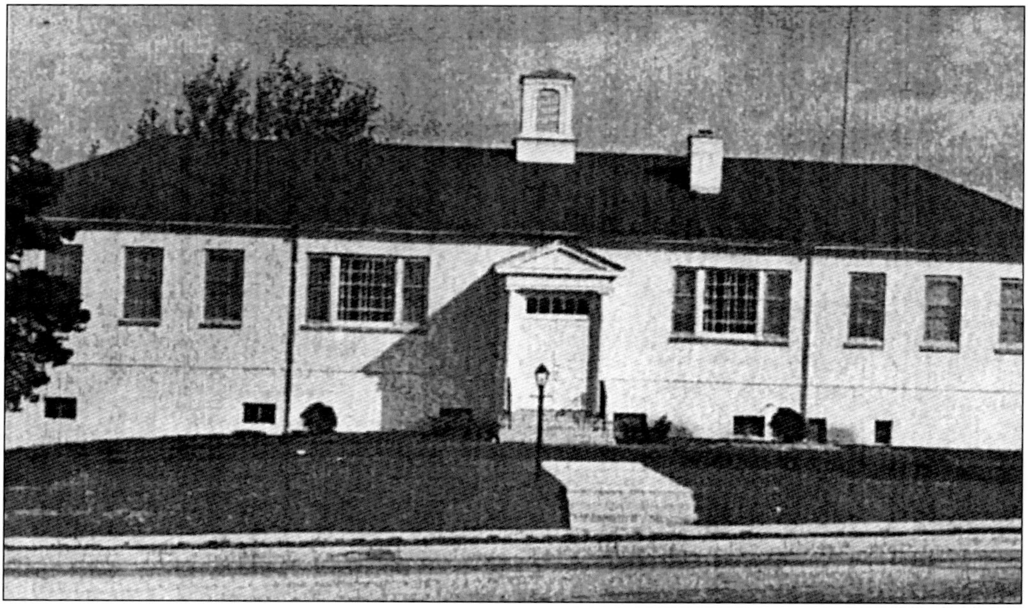

The Marple Township Municipal Building stood at Sproul and Springfield Roads until 1976, when the present municipal building and library were constructed on the site. (Marple Newtown Historical Society.)

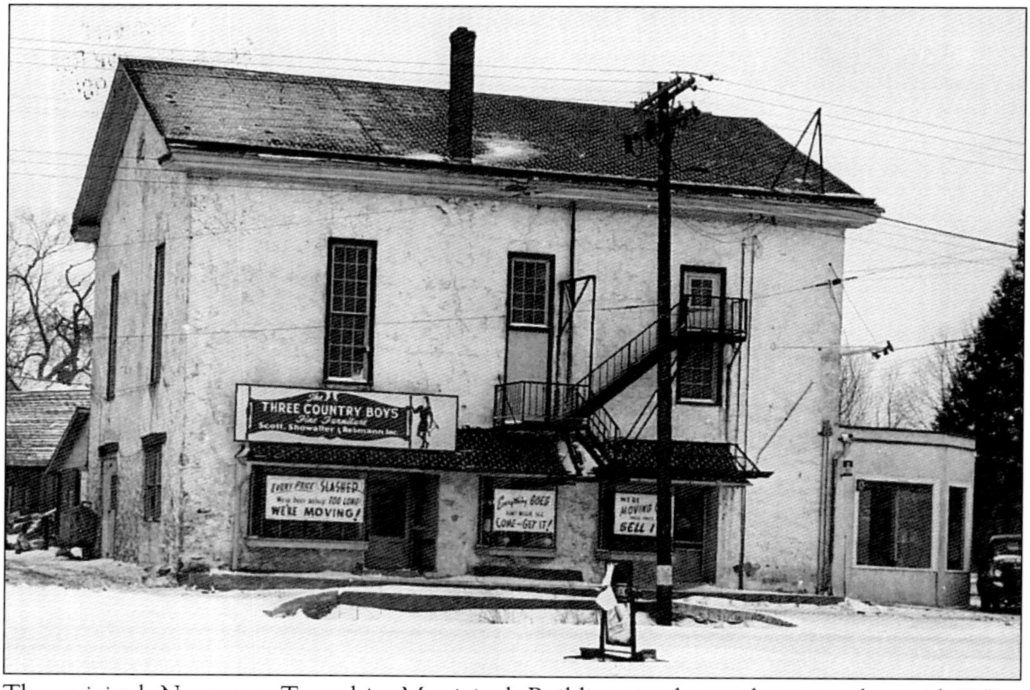

The original Newtown Township Municipal Building is shown here in the mid-1950s. (Seth Pancoast.)

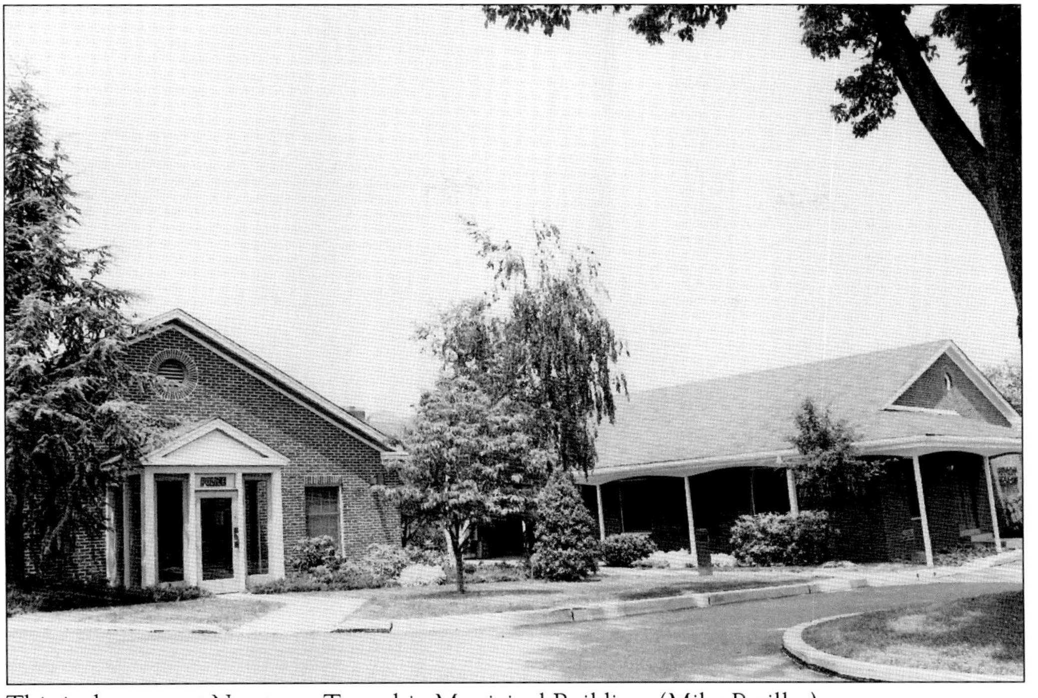

This is the present Newtown Township Municipal Building. (Mike Perillo.)

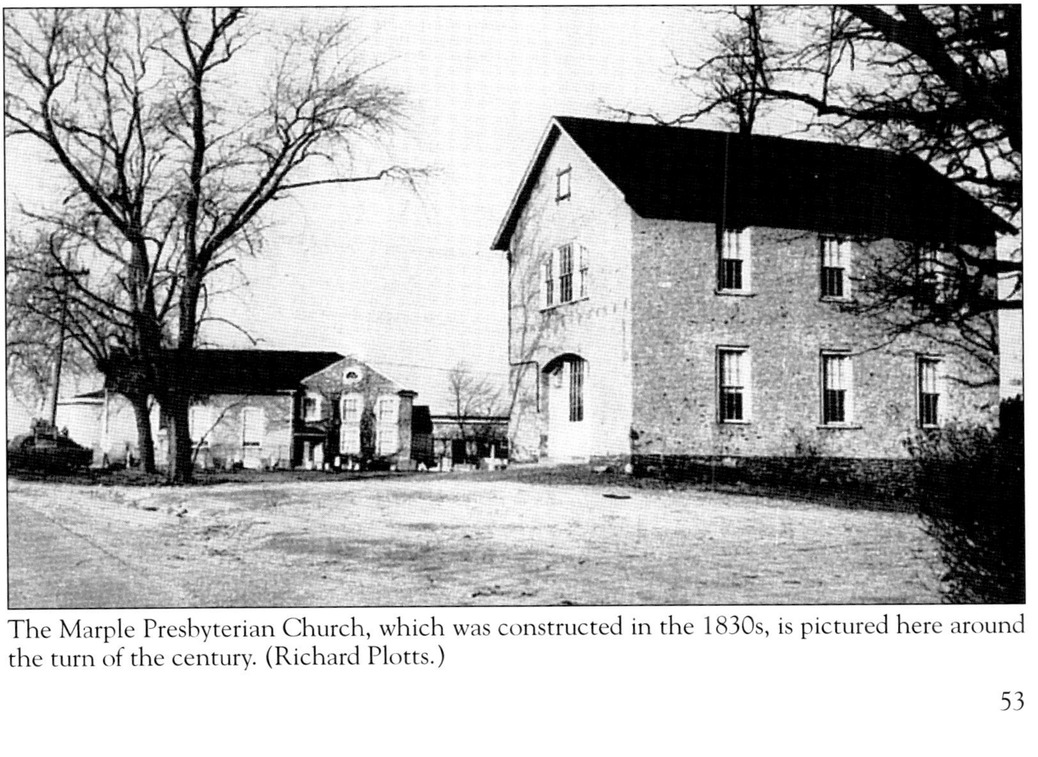

The Marple Presbyterian Church, which was constructed in the 1830s, is pictured here around the turn of the century. (Richard Plotts.)

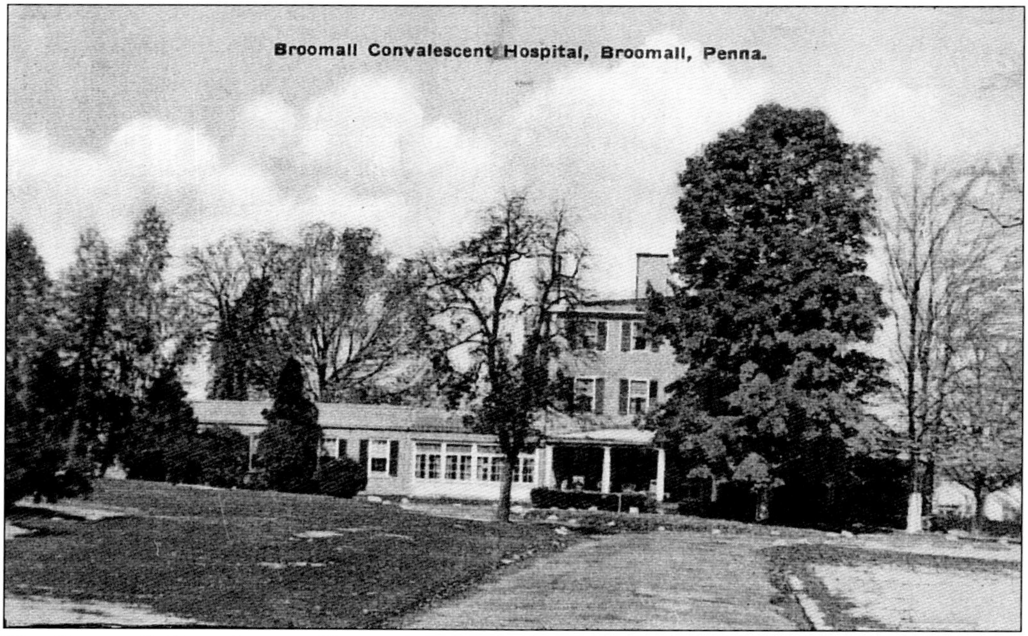

The Broomall Convalescent Hospital was one of several institutions developed to expose city residents to the benefits of fresh country air and clean water. (Richard Plotts.)

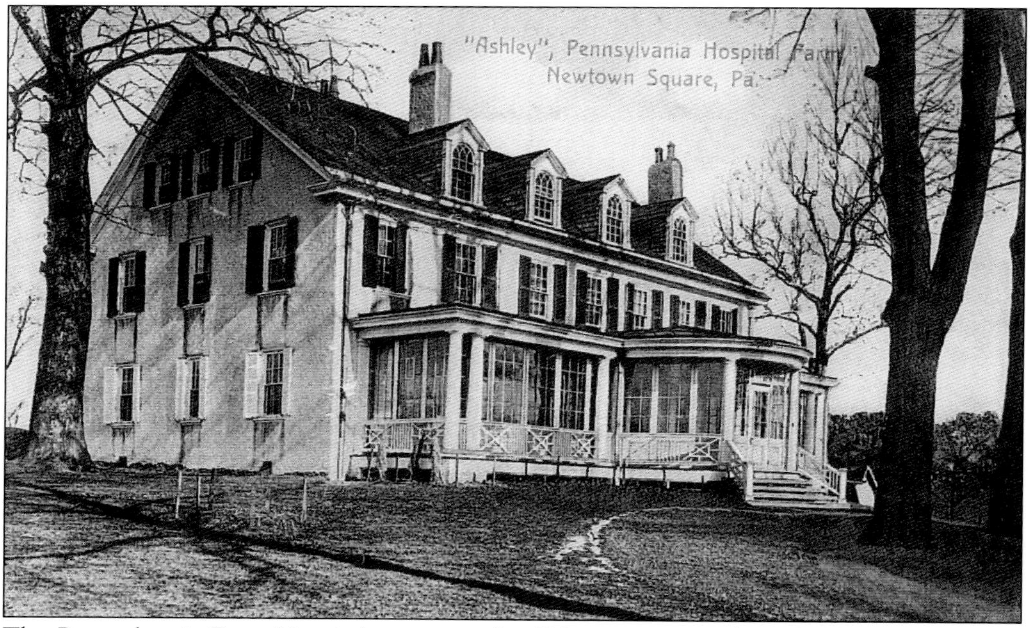

The Pennsylvania Farm Hospital was part of a 600-acre property bounded by West Chester Pike and Route 252. Mental patients were cared for on the property, which later became the Dowden Nursing Home. (Richard Plotts.)

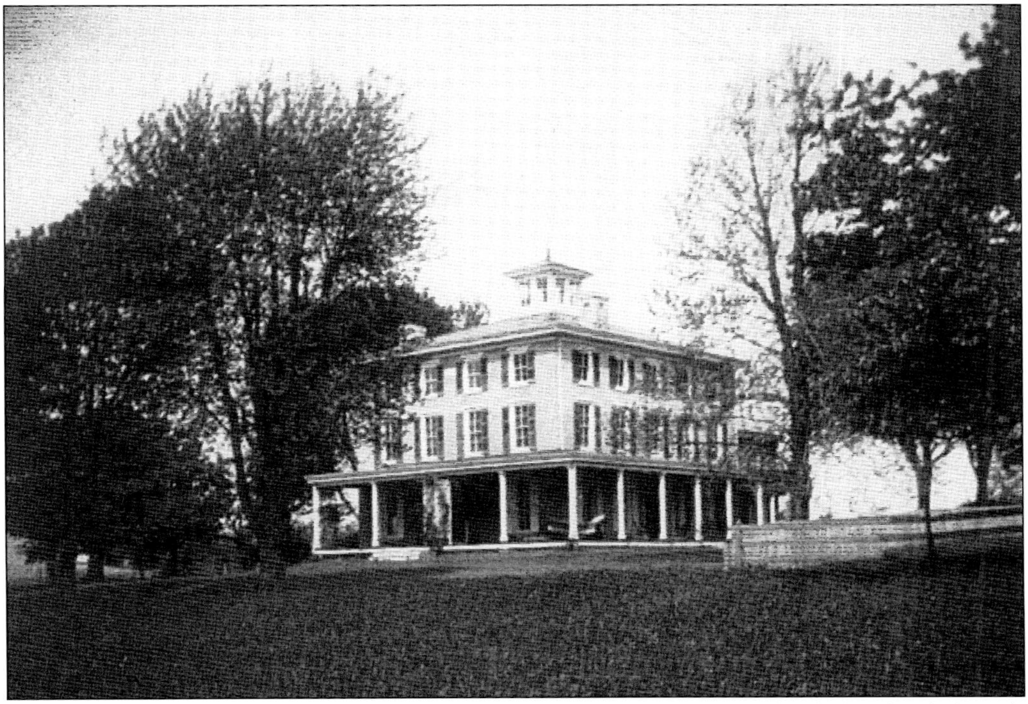

The Greenland Estate was located on the grounds of the former Ellis School. (Richard Plotts.)

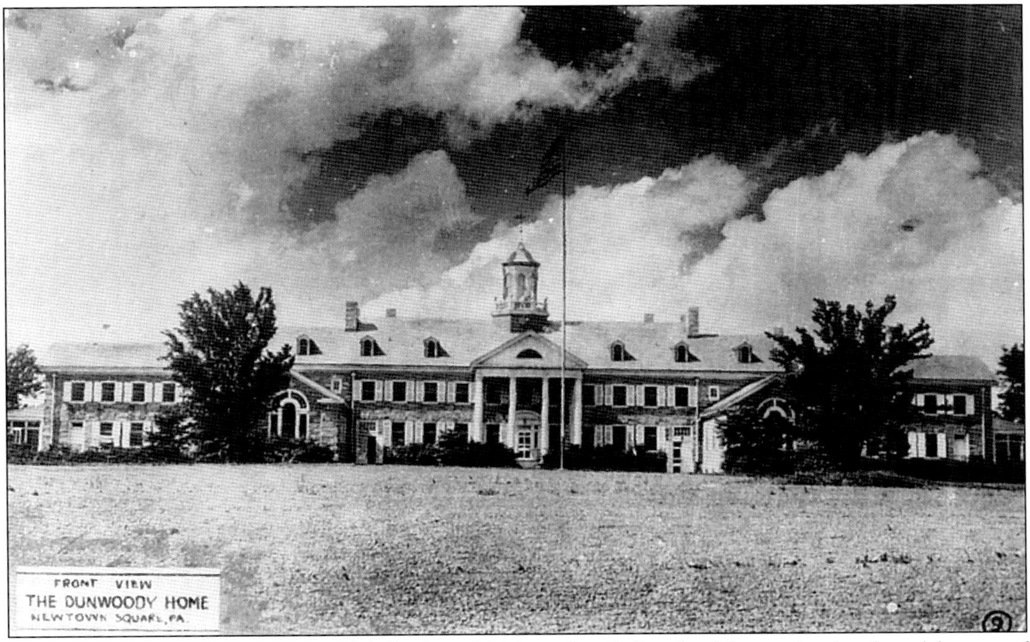

The Dunwoody Home was established in 1924 on land that had been the boyhood home of William Hood Dunwoody. He bequeathed $1 million in 1913 to establish the home for senior citizens. (Richard Plotts.)

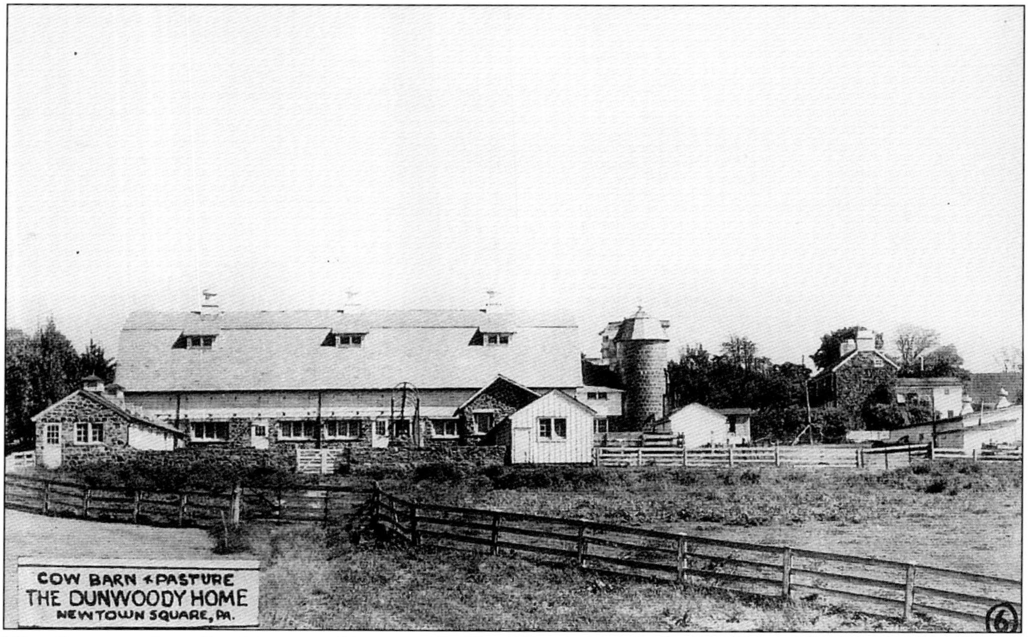

The farms and outbuildings at Dunwoody Home are pictured here. Farming was discontinued on the property in 1957. (Richard Plotts.)

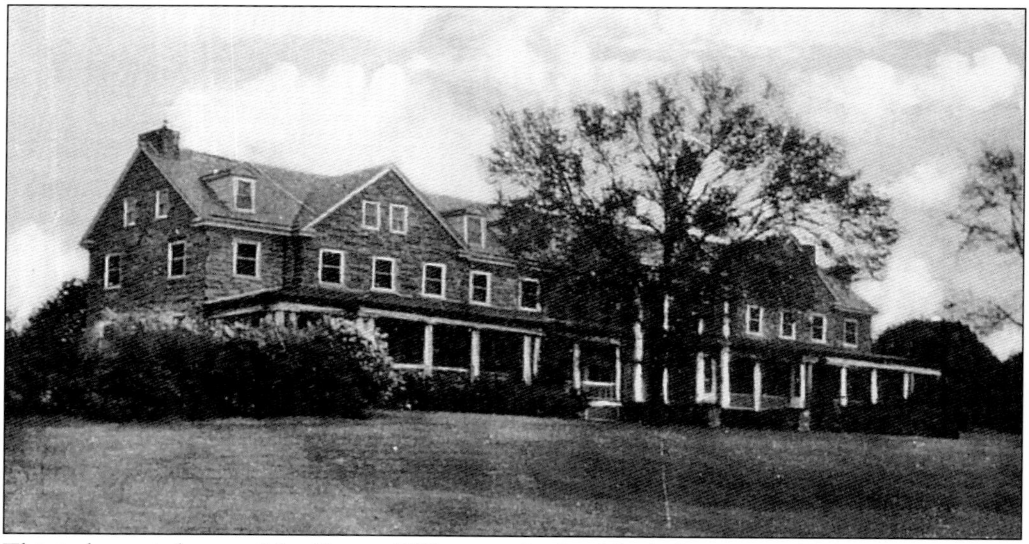

This is the main house of the Garrett Williamson Lodge. The lodge was established on the former Williamson Farm as a vacation home for poor children and single women from Philadelphia and other communities where farm life was not known. (Richard Plotts.)

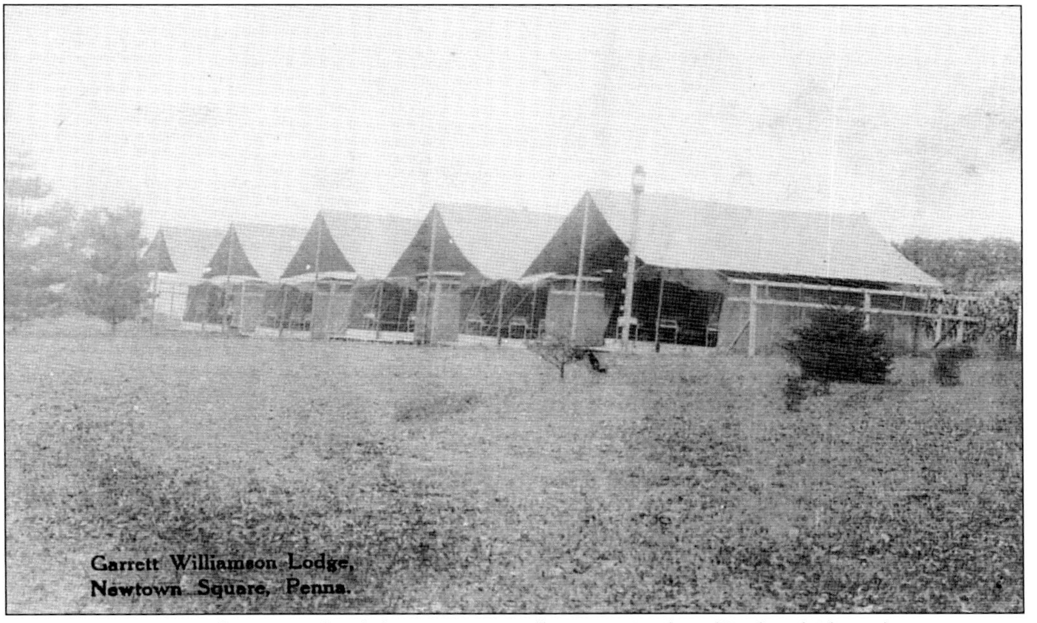

These are tents on the grounds of the Garrett Williamson Lodge. (Richard Plotts.)

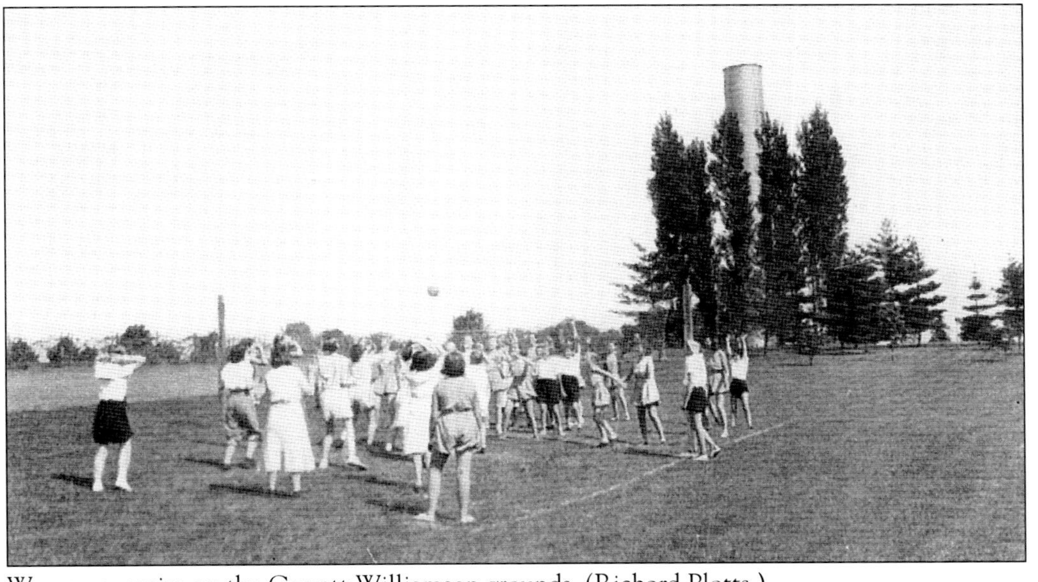
Women exercise on the Garrett Williamson grounds. (Richard Plotts.)

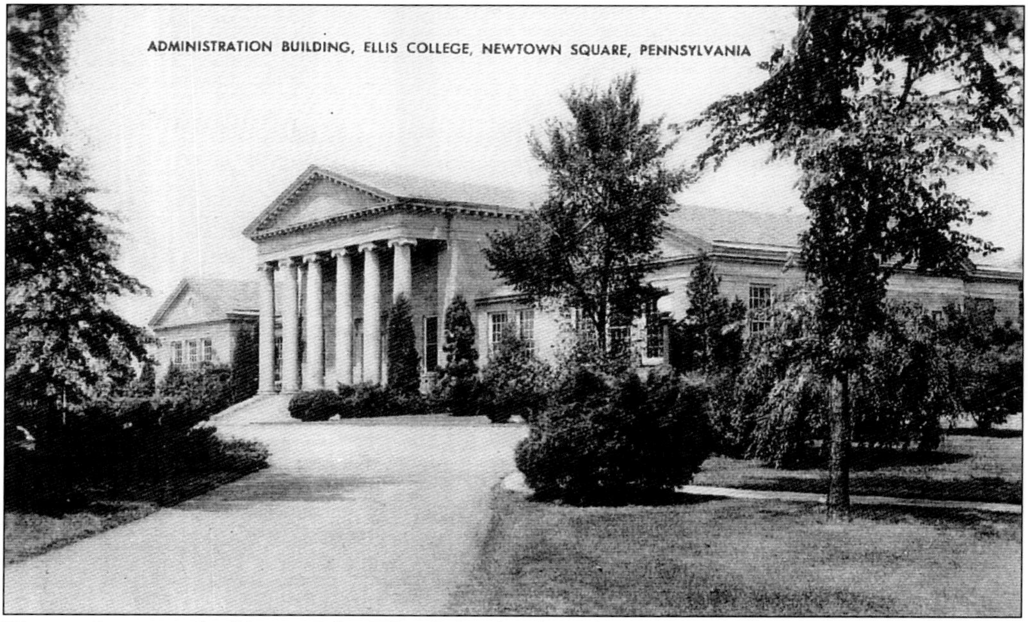

This is the main building of the Ellis School. The school was for fatherless girls and it was established by the will of Philadelphia philanthropist Charles Ellis in 1919. The school closed in 1977. (Richard Plotts.)

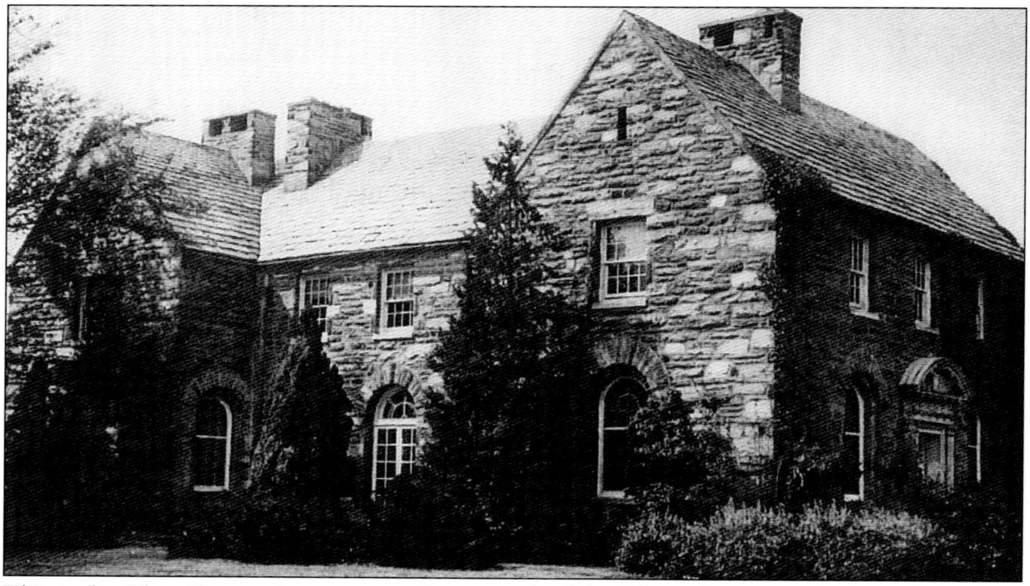

This is the Clara Barton dormitory on the grounds of the Ellis School. (Richard Plotts.)

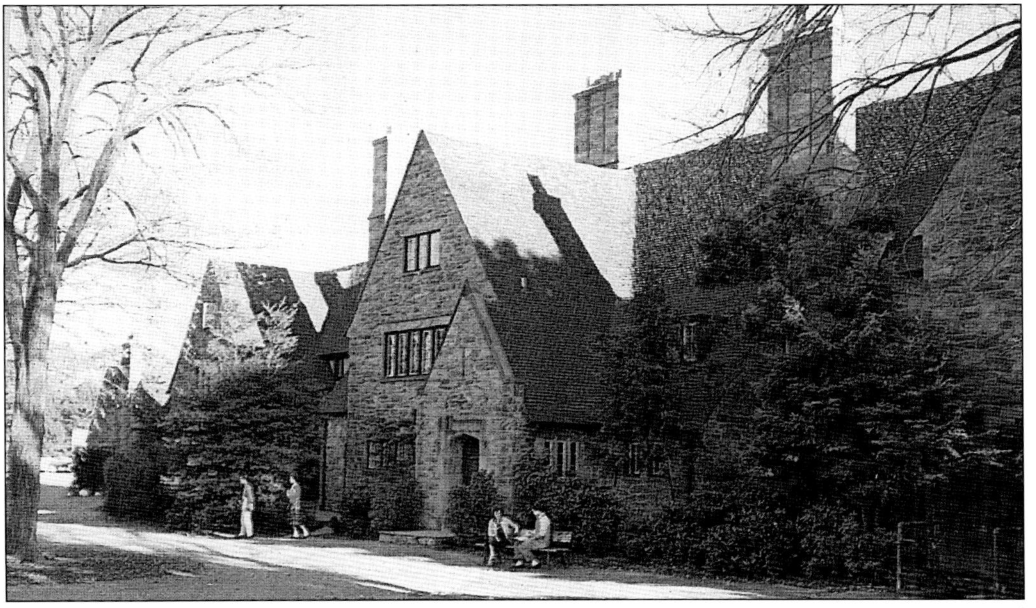

This is the main building of the Delaware County Christian School, which was incorporated in 1950 by a small group of Christian families. In addition to buildings on the 11-acre former Strawbridge Estate on Malin Road, the school also has a campus in the former Alice Grimm School. (Richard Plotts.)

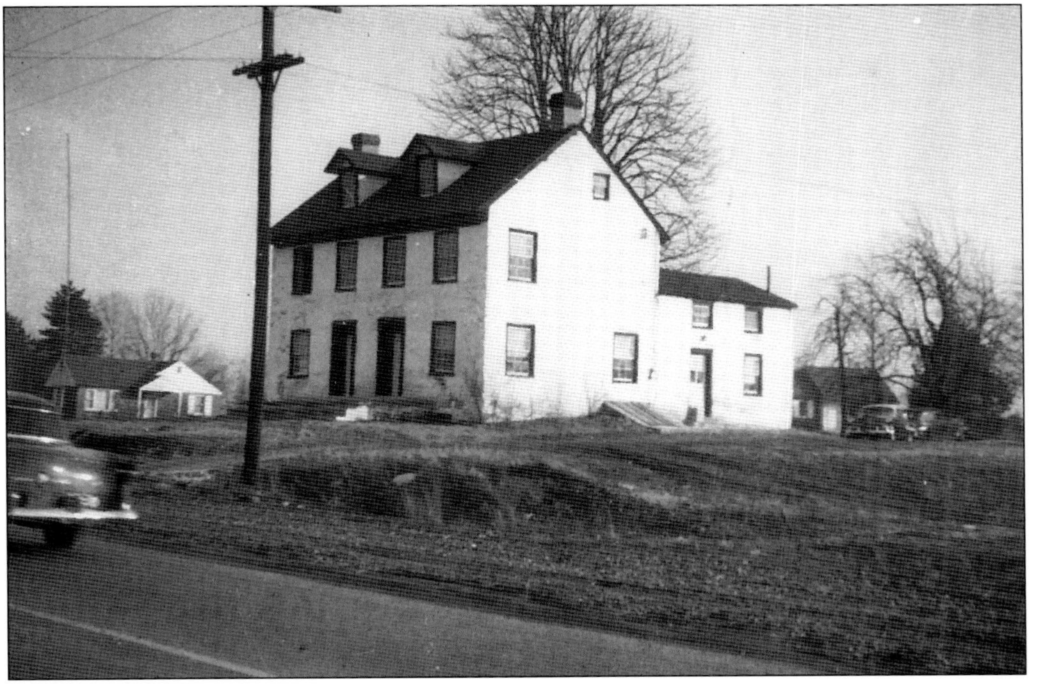

This home, shown here in the 1940s, was located on the site new occupied by the American Legion hall on West Chester Pike. (Hilda Lucas.)

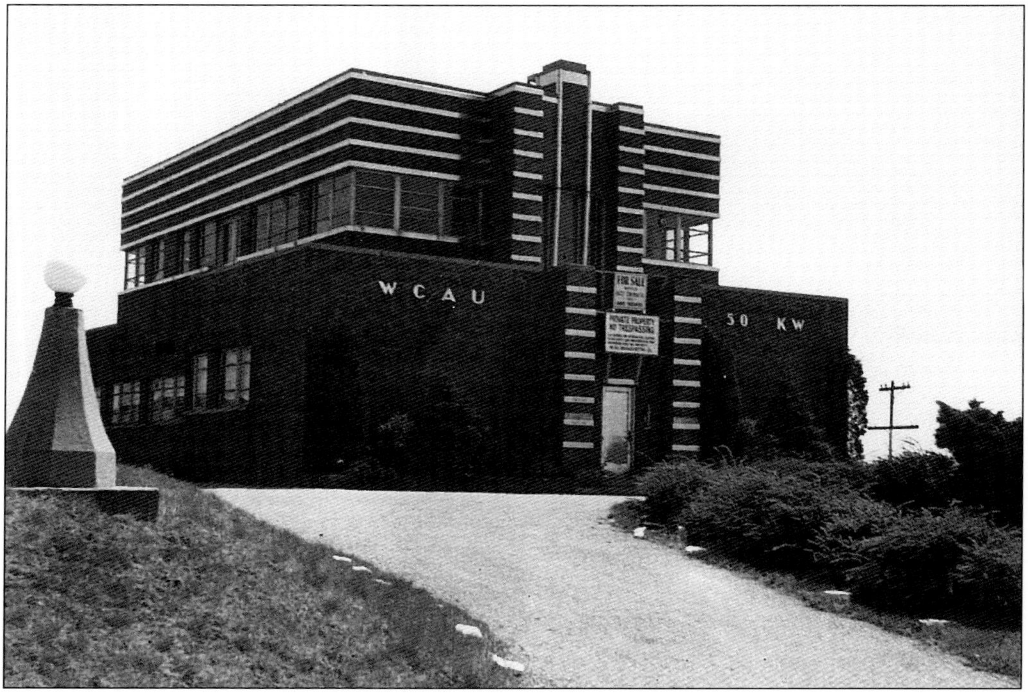

The WCAU radio transmission building on Bishop Hollow Road across from the Garrett Williamson property was erected in 1931 to accommodate an increase in the station's power. The site closed in August 1941. (Seth Pancoast.)

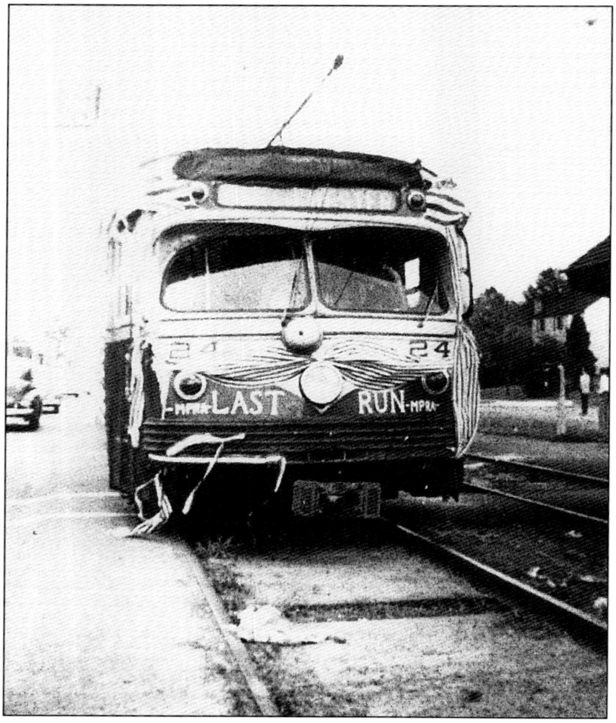

The front of the trolley that ran from Philadelphia to West Chester is pictured here on its last day of operation on June 4, 1954. The trolley line was replaced by buses, which continue to run today. (Seth Pancoast.)

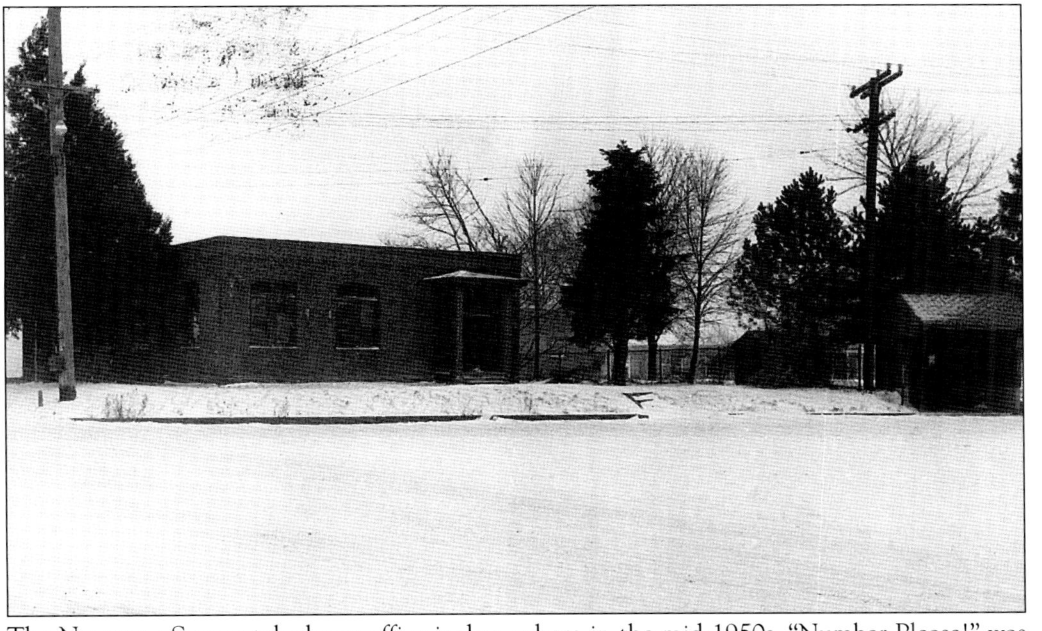

The Newtown Square telephone office is shown here in the mid-1950s. "Number Please!" was the standard phrase heard when one would lift the telephone receiver prior to February 1954. On that date the dial system became effective with the Elgin exchange, known simply as 353, 356, or 359 today. (Seth Pancoast.)

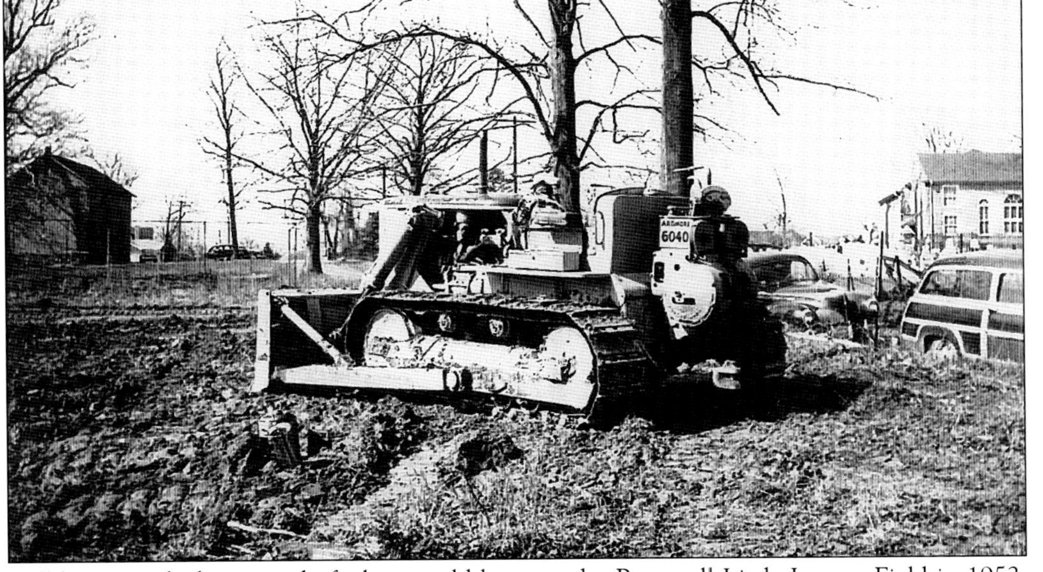

Bulldozers work the ground of what would become the Broomall Little League Field in 1952. (Seth Pancoast.)

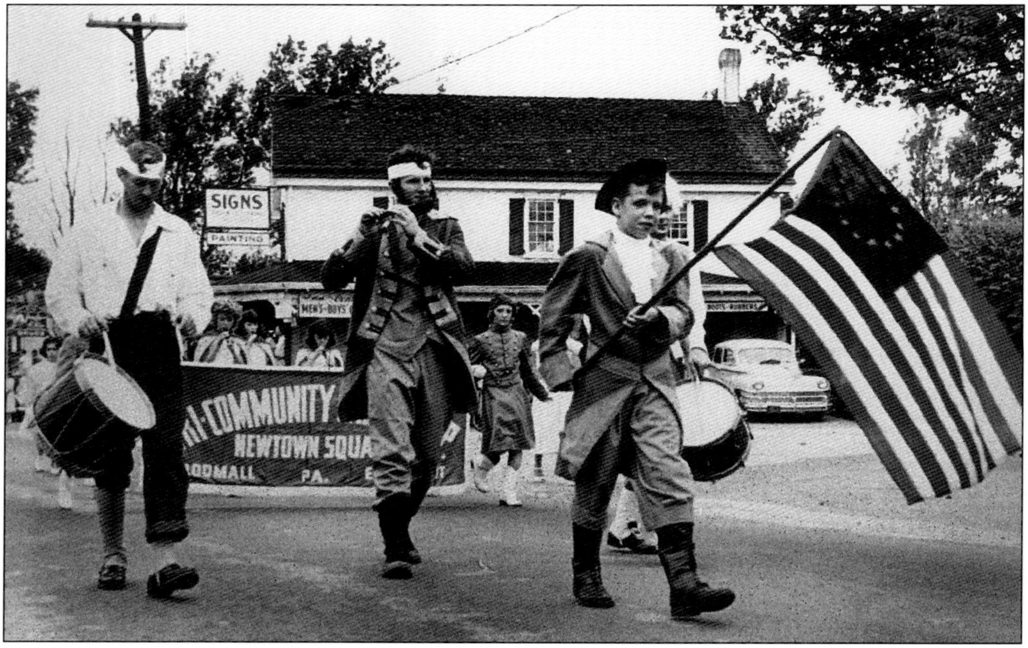

The Community Drum and Bugle Corps march in a Marple Newtown Fourth of July parade in the 1940s. (Bill Greco and Jan Ceton.)

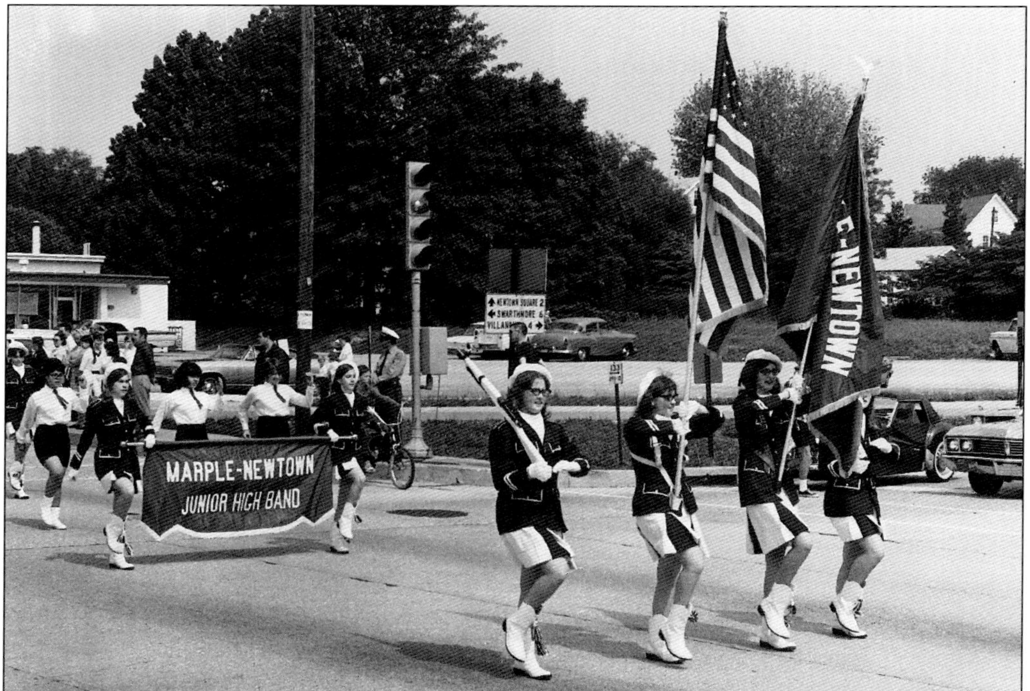

The Marple Newtown Junior High School Band is shown here in the 1960s. (Bill Greco.)

Five

PEOPLE

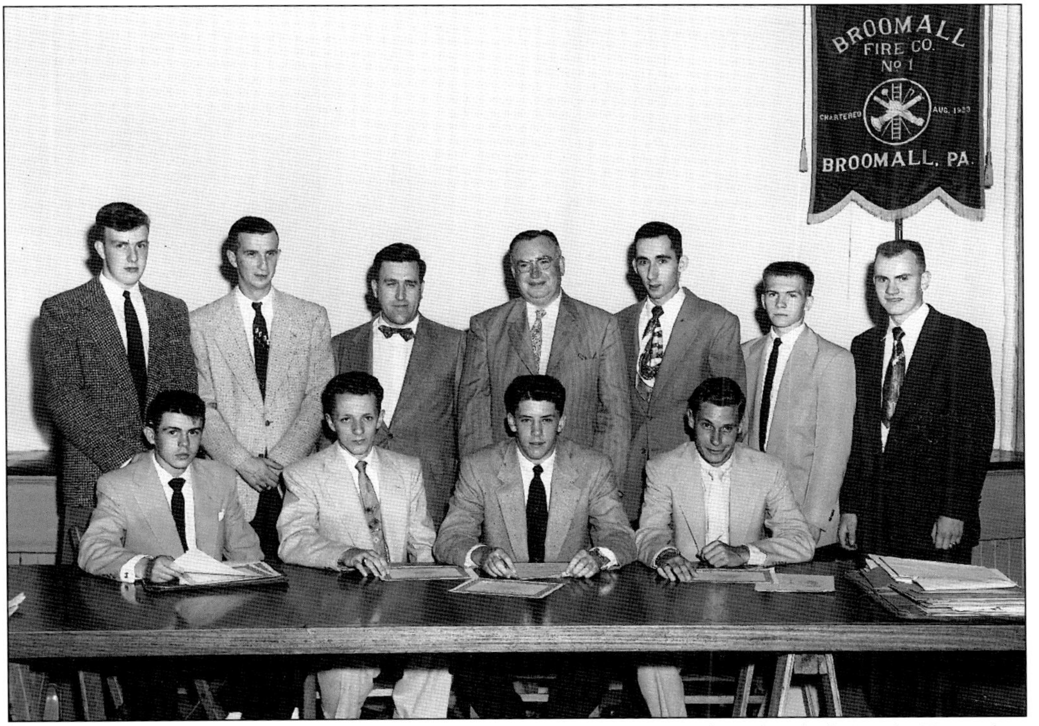

This is the 1954 student government of Marple Newtown High School. (Marple Township Police Department.)

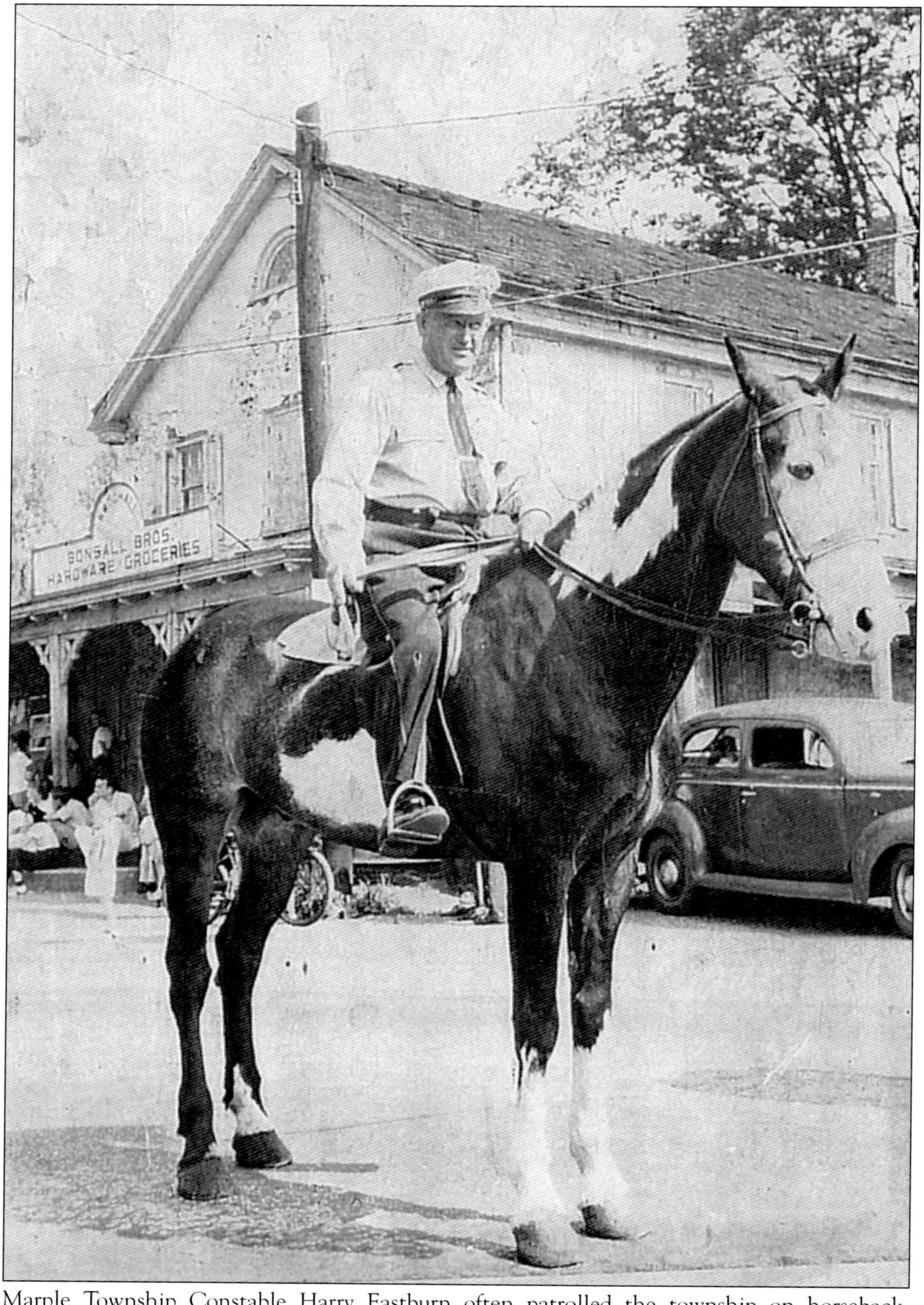

Marple Township Constable Harry Eastburn often patrolled the township on horseback. (Dick Standen.)

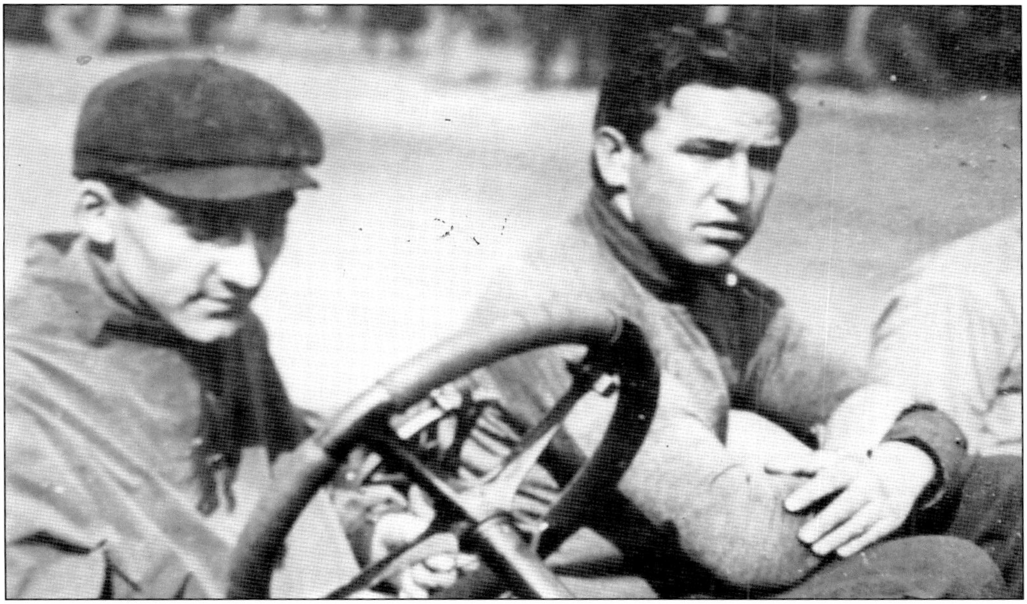

The Bergdoll brothers pose in one of their racecars. (Hilda Lucas.)

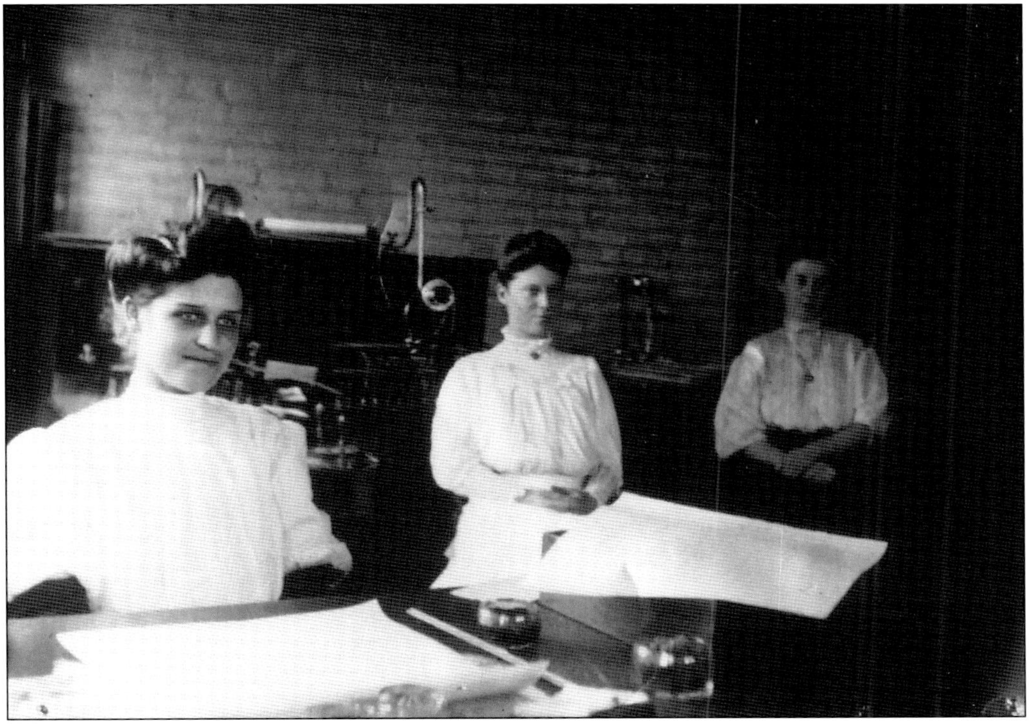

Telephone operators manned the Bell Telephone office in Newtown Square in 1906. (Hilda Lucas.)

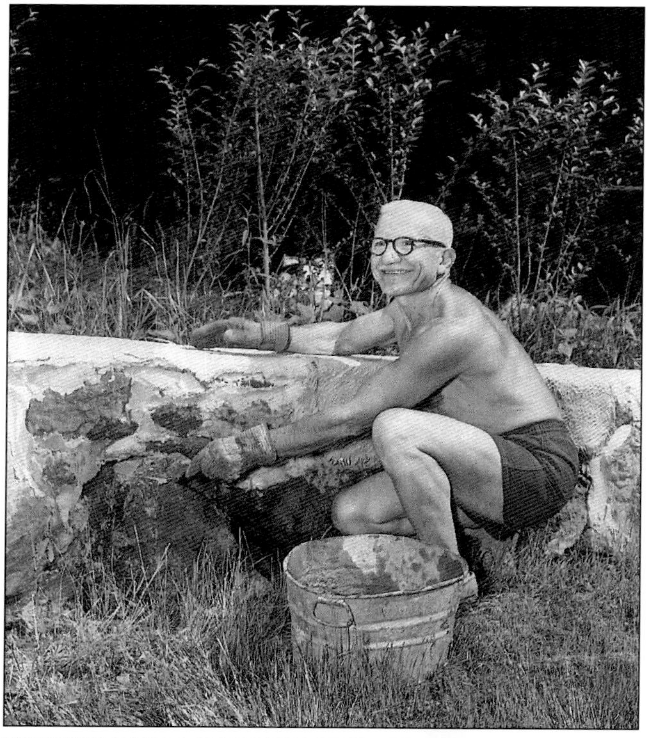

Dr. Vram Neudurian worked at his Newtown summer home, which was situated between Malley, Morton, Third, and Fourth Streets. Neudurian was a Philadelphia physician who bought the Newtown property in 1927. The Red Cross gave swimming and CPR lessons at the pool, and no one drowned or contracted polio. (Pam Kitabjian.)

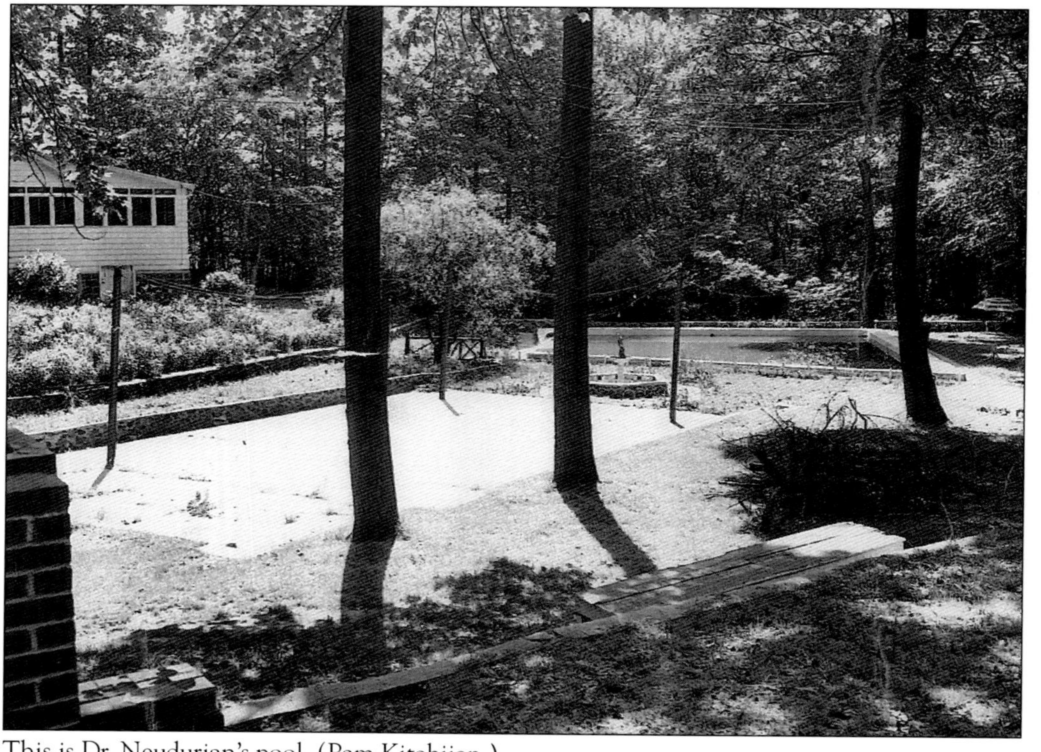

This is Dr. Neudurian's pool. (Pam Kitabjian.)

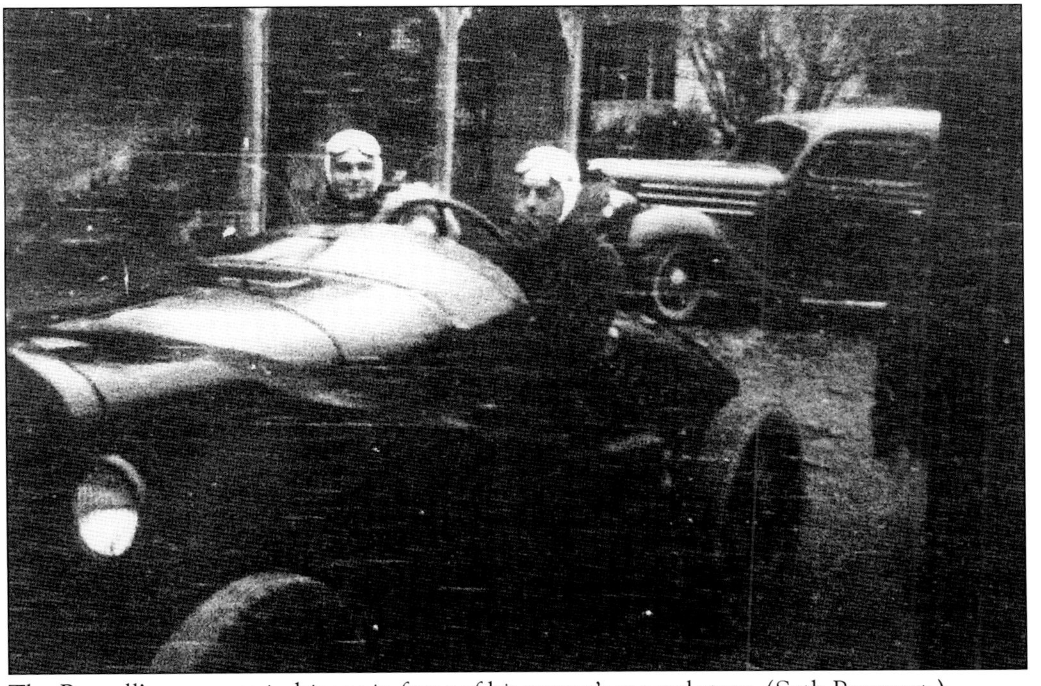

The Bonsall's son poses in his car in front of his parent's general store. (Seth Pancoast.)

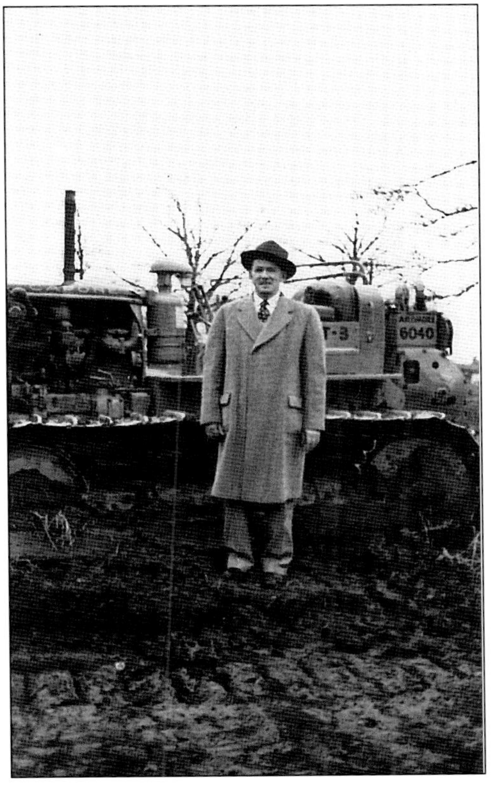

Seth Pancoast Sr. was a respected businessman who was involved in many endeavors and community projects. This photograph was taken in 1952, when he was involved in construction of the Broomall Little League field. (Seth Pancoast.)

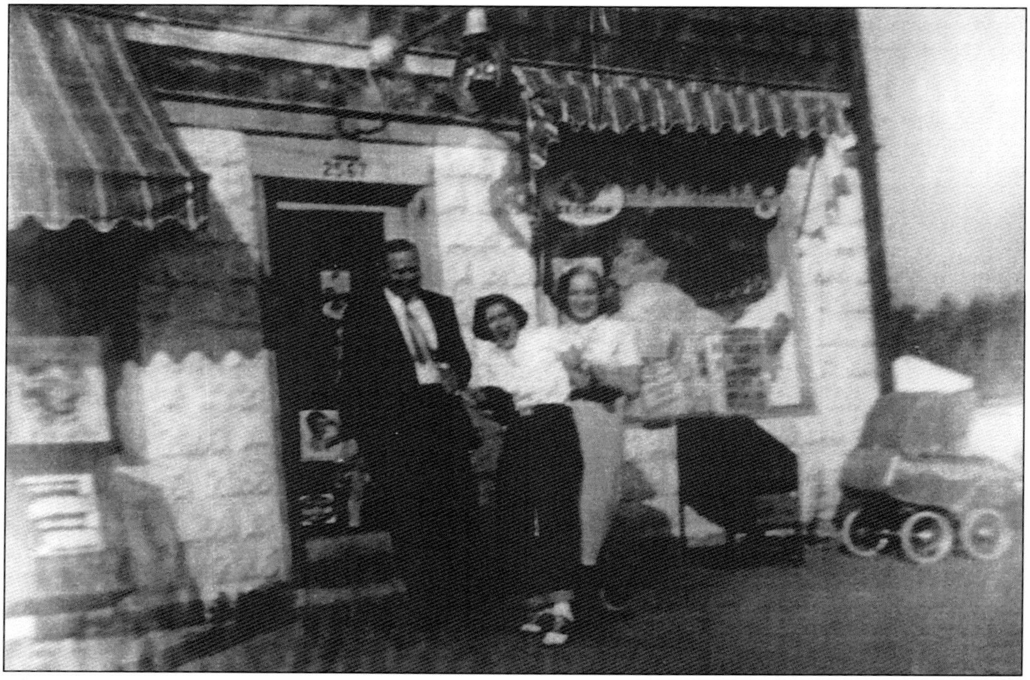

Three people pose in front of Bessie Parker's store in 1954. (John Kuseian.)

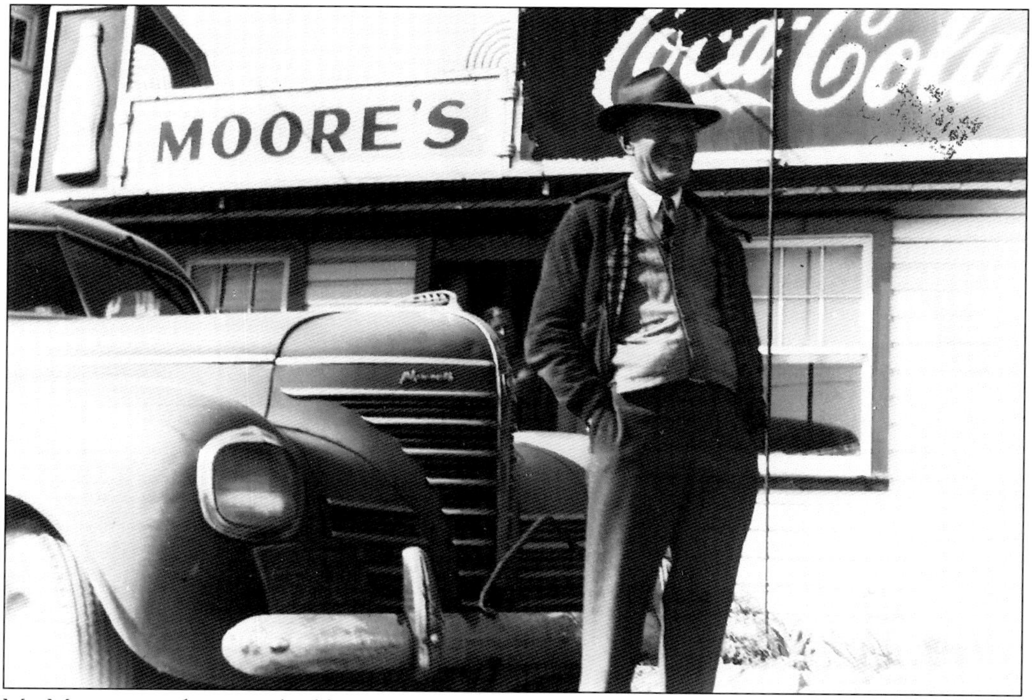

Mr. Moore was photographed here in front of his luncheonette. (Al Vandetty.)

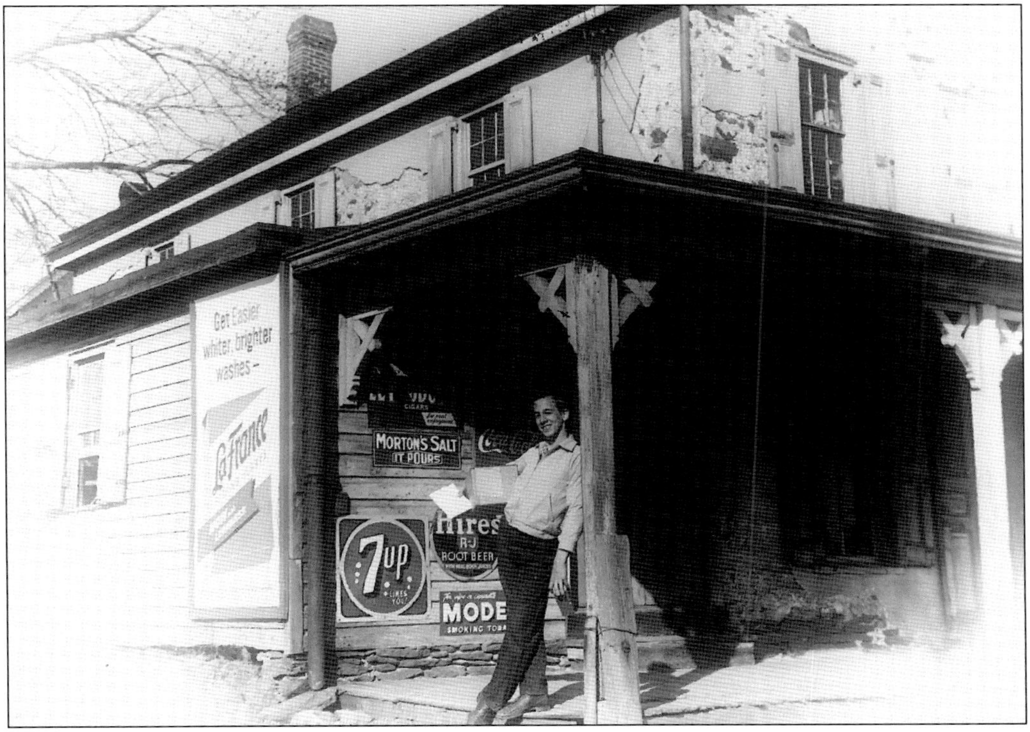

An unidentified man stands on the front porch of Bonsall's store. (Seth Pancoast.)

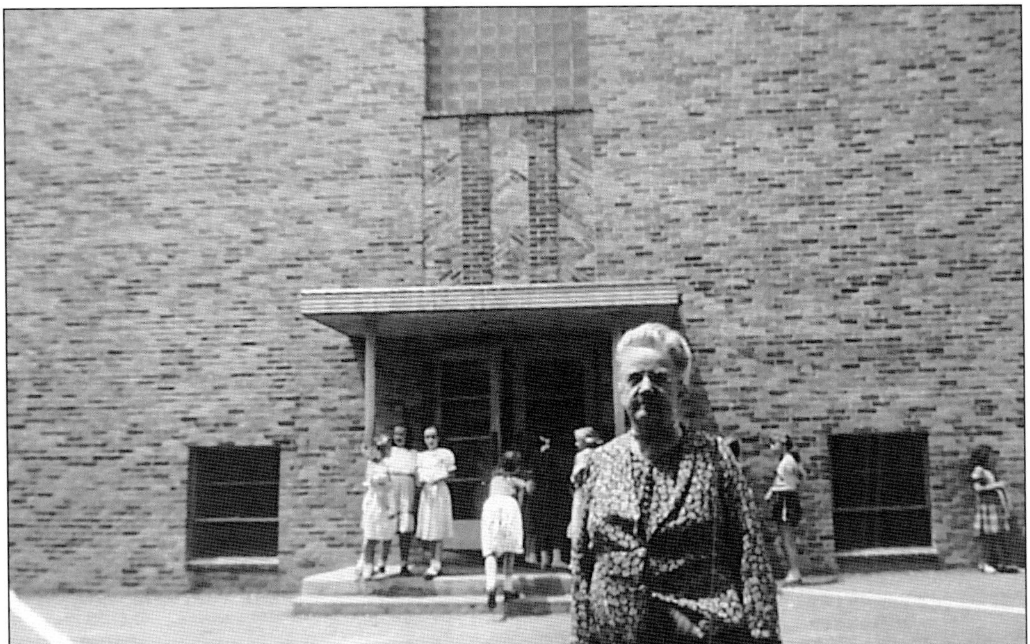
Miss South was one of the most popular teachers at the Marple School in the 1940s and 1950s. (Jan Ceton.)

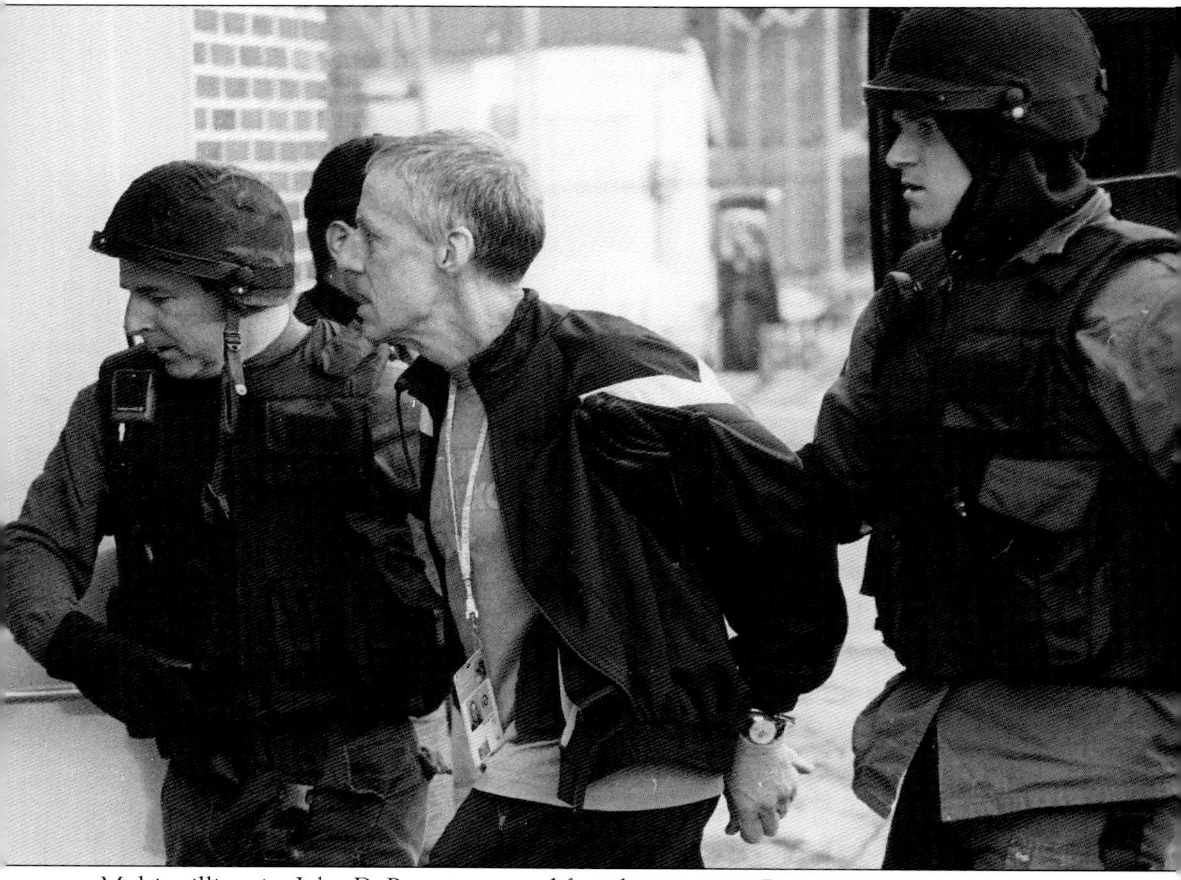

Multi-millionaire John DuPont is escorted from his estate on Route 252 in Newtown by police following a 24-hour standoff that began after DuPont shot and killed Olympic wrestler David Schultz. DuPont was convicted of the killing. (Mike Perillo.)

Six

Having Fun

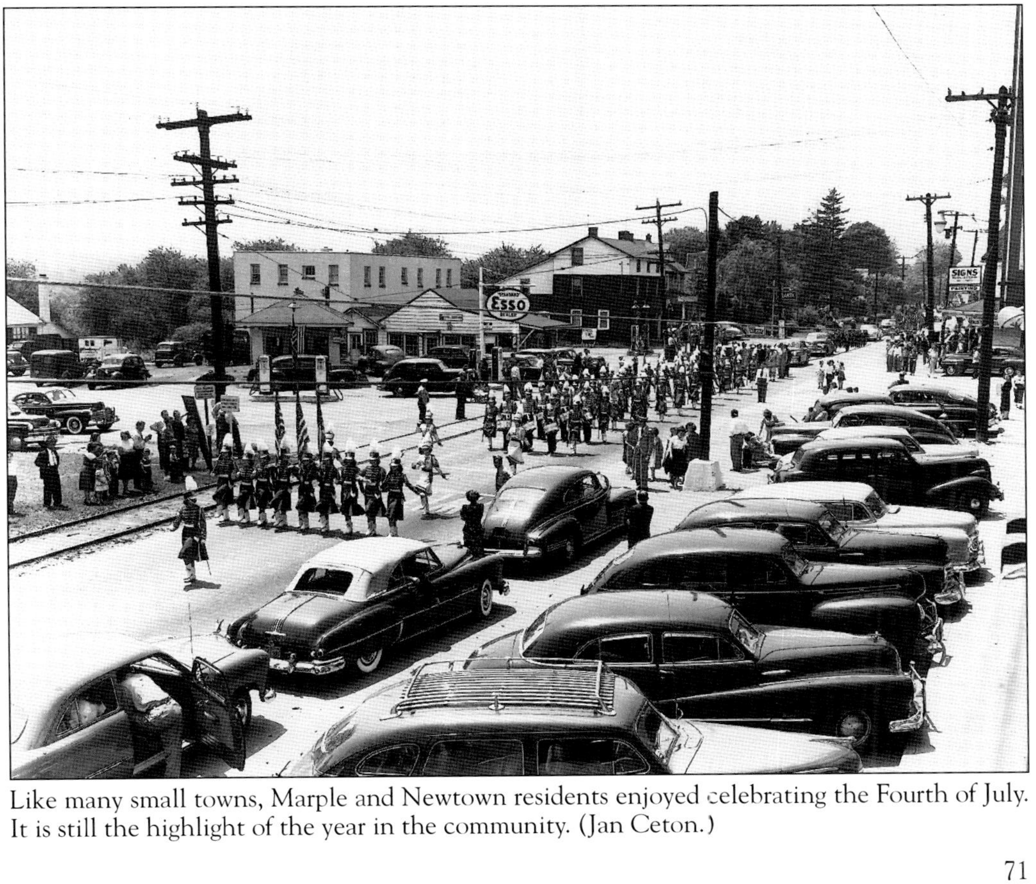

Like many small towns, Marple and Newtown residents enjoyed celebrating the Fourth of July. It is still the highlight of the year in the community. (Jan Ceton.)

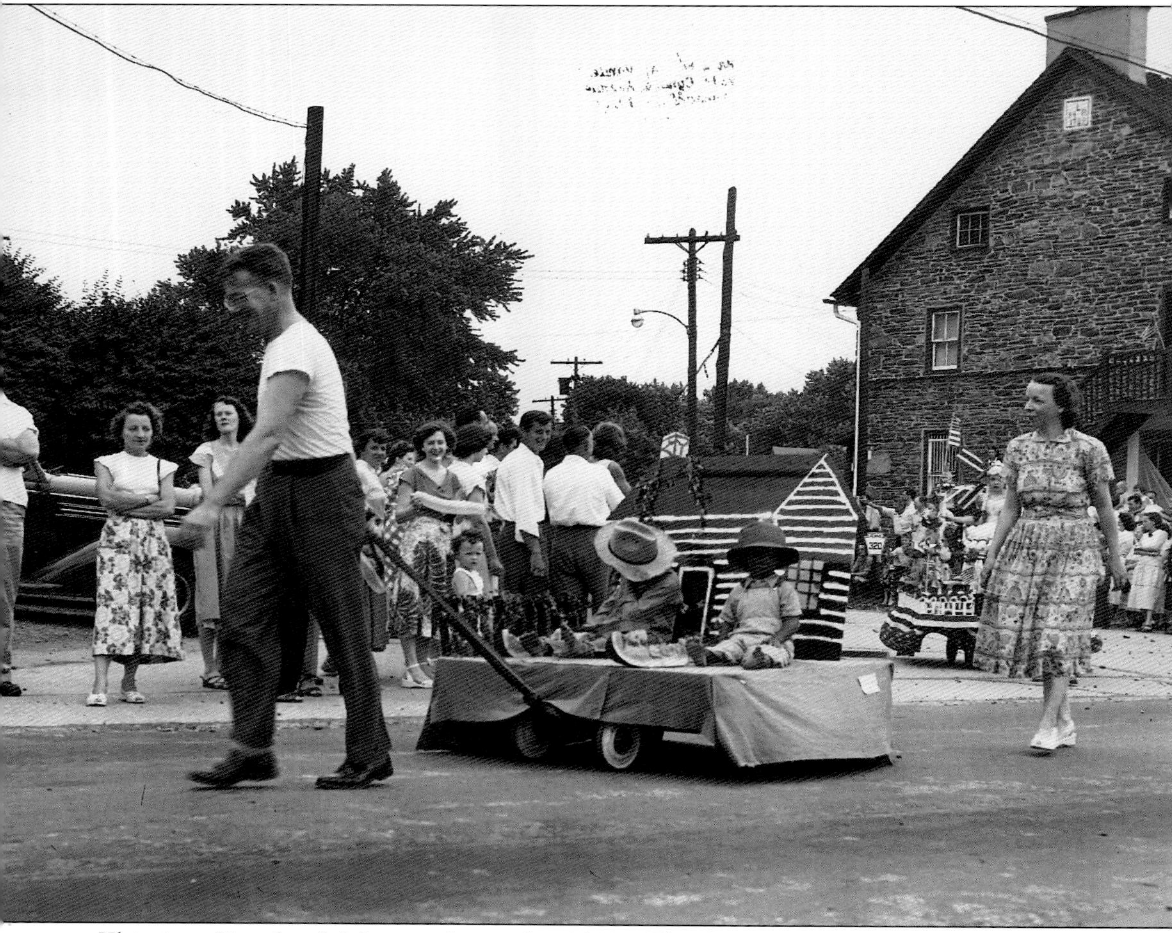

This is a Fourth of July parade in the 1940s. The Drove Tavern is in the foreground. (Al Vandetty.)

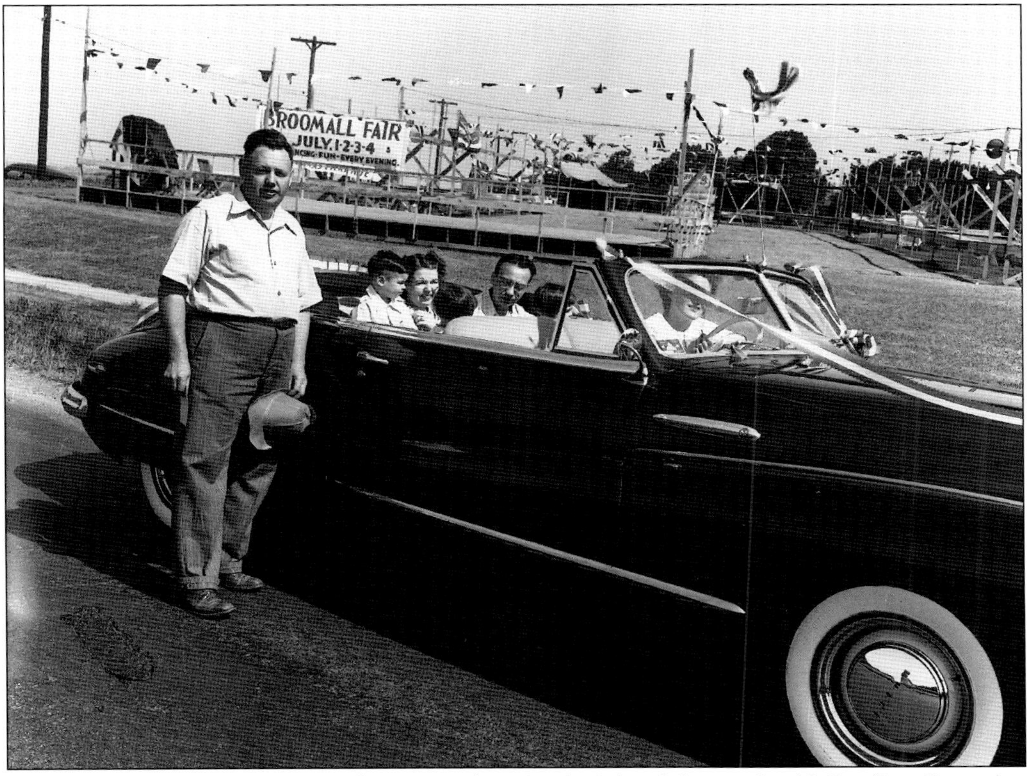

The Broomall Fair was an annual event at the Marple School during the 1940s. (Jan Ceton.)

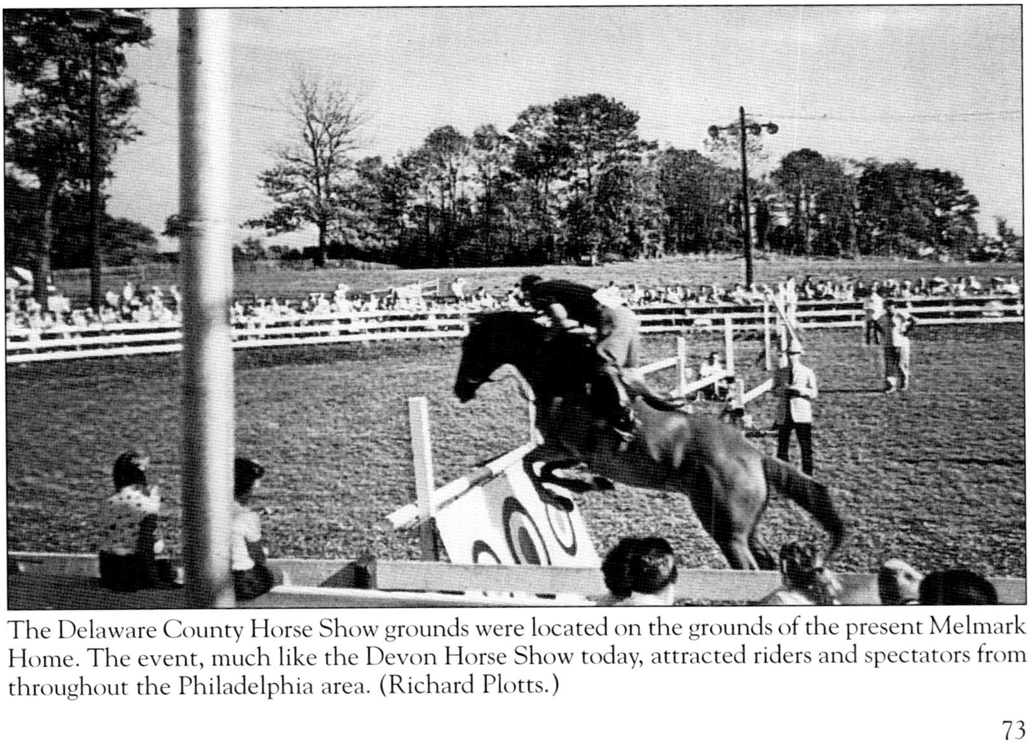
The Delaware County Horse Show grounds were located on the grounds of the present Melmark Home. The event, much like the Devon Horse Show today, attracted riders and spectators from throughout the Philadelphia area. (Richard Plotts.)

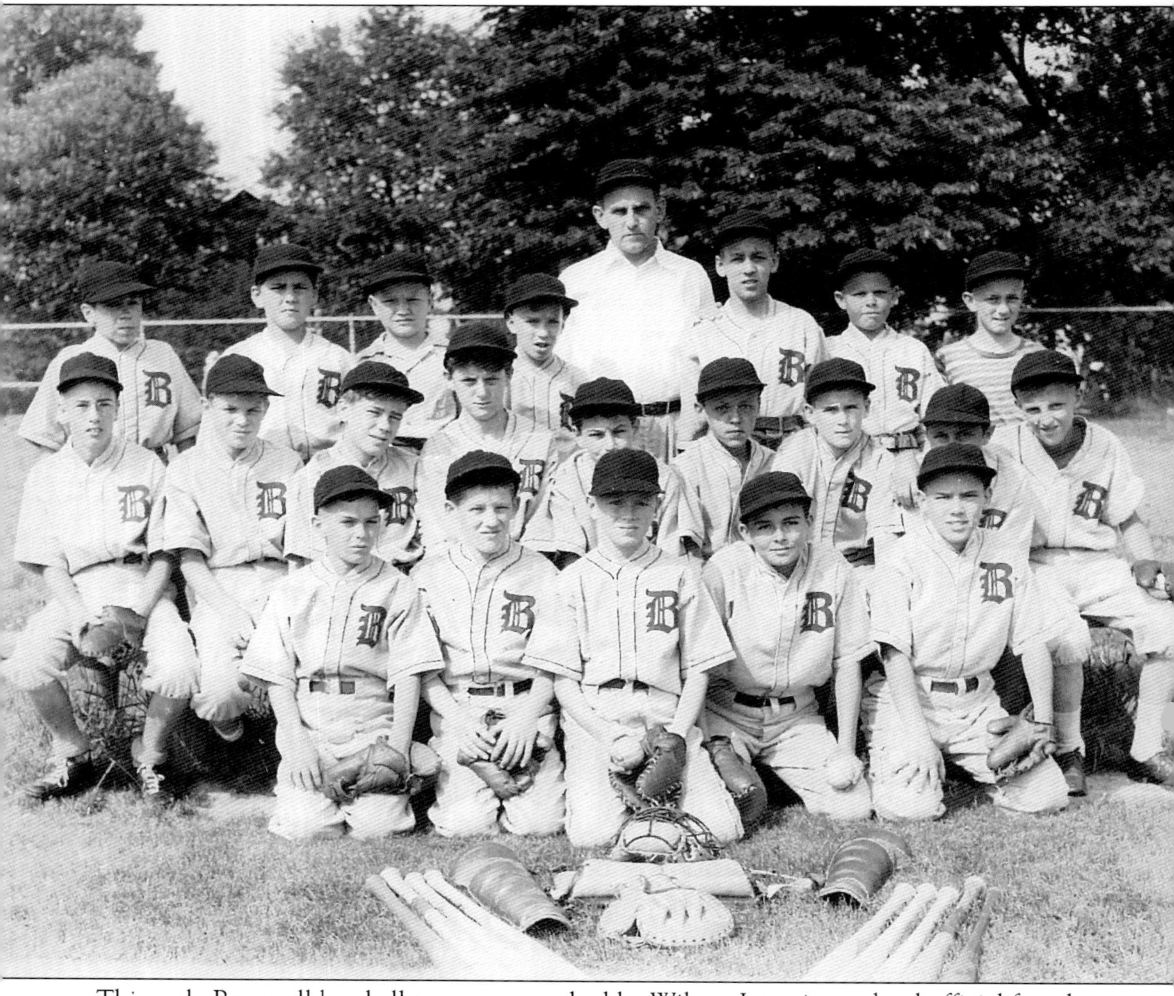

This early Broomall baseball team was coached by Wilmer Loomis, a school official for whom the Loomis Elementary School is named. (Seth Pancoast.)

Seven

SUBURBAN SPRAWL

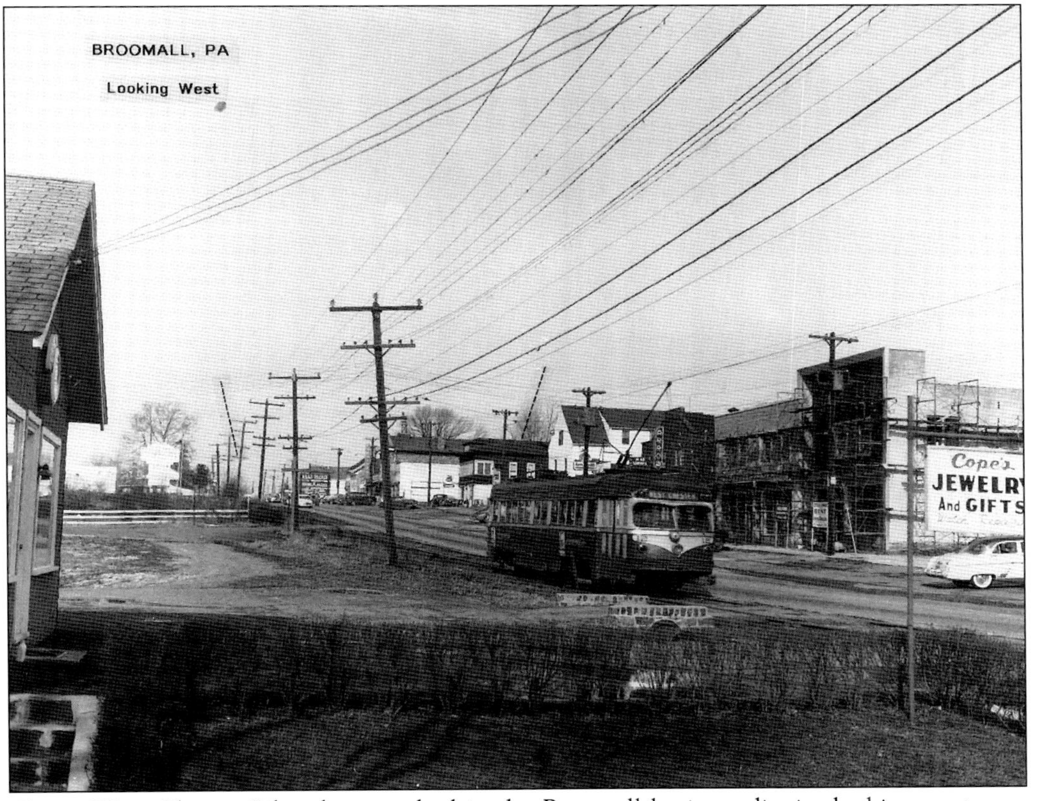

This is West Chester Pike photographed in the Broomall business district looking west near Alameda Road in the 1940s. (John Kuseian.)

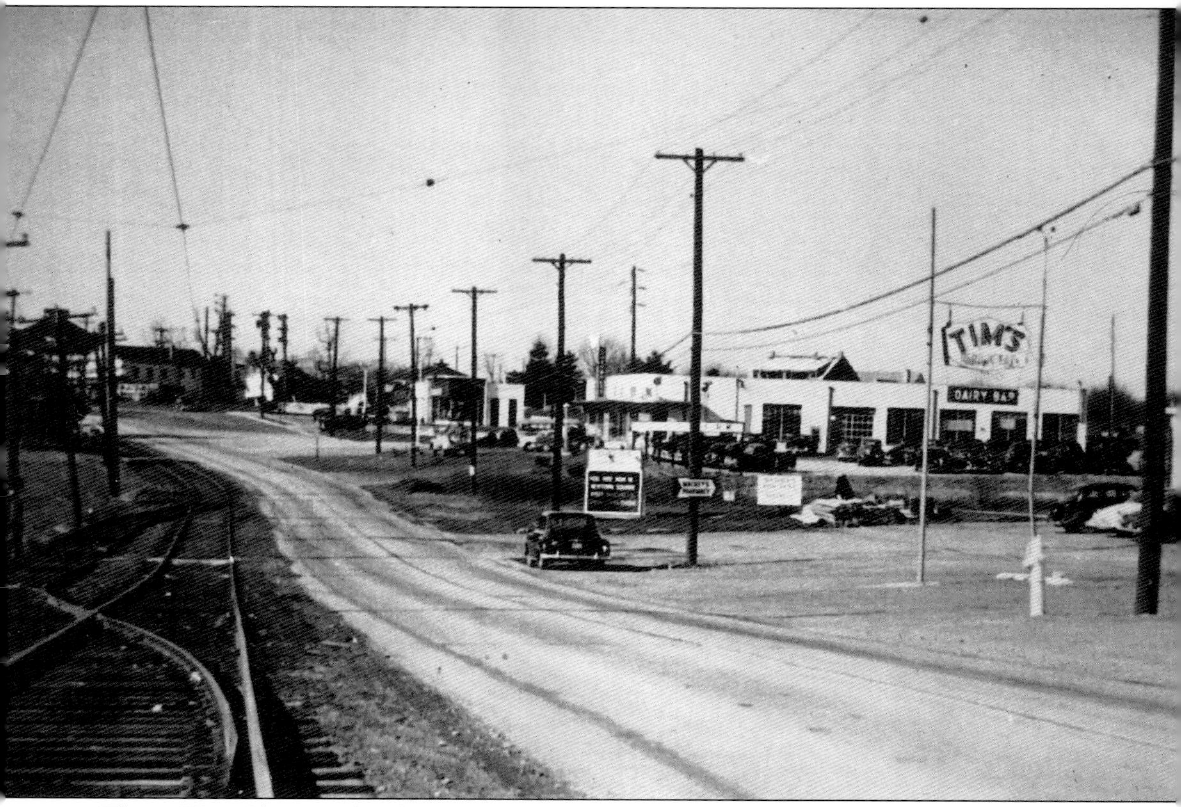

This is West Chester Pike photographed in the Newtown Square business district in the 1940s. (Hilda Lucas.)

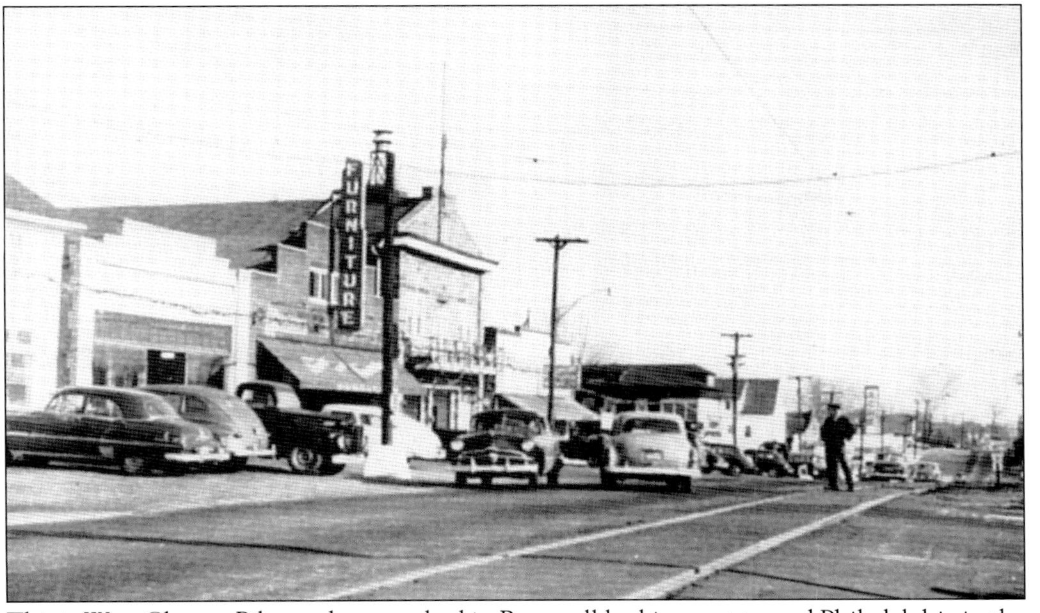

This is West Chester Pike as photographed in Broomall looking east toward Philadelphia in the 1950s. (Richard Plotts.)

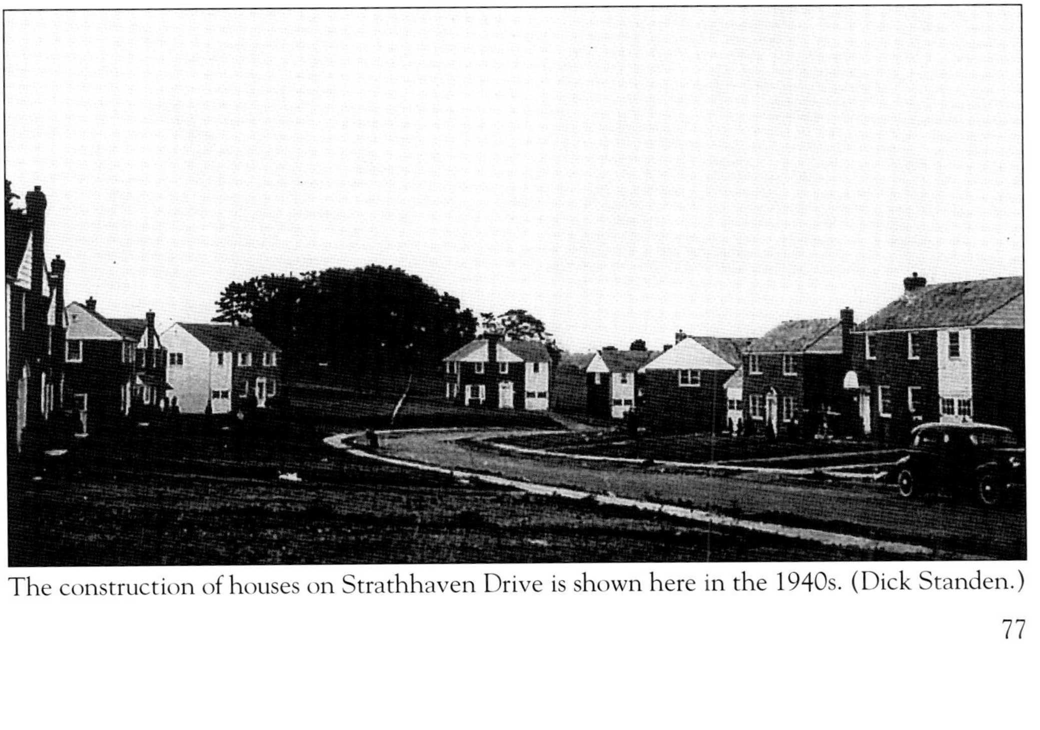

The construction of houses on Strathhaven Drive is shown here in the 1940s. (Dick Standen.)

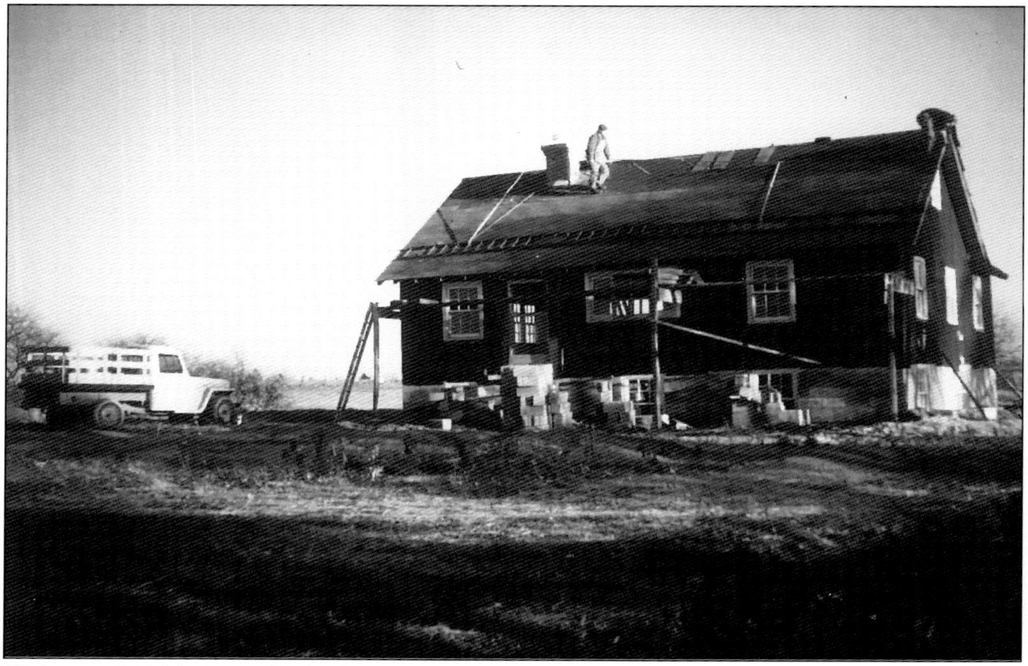

Walter and Hilda Lucas built their house on Lewis Road in 1948. The house was the first on the street and the field behind it is now the home of St. Mark's United Methodist Church. (Hilda Lucas.)

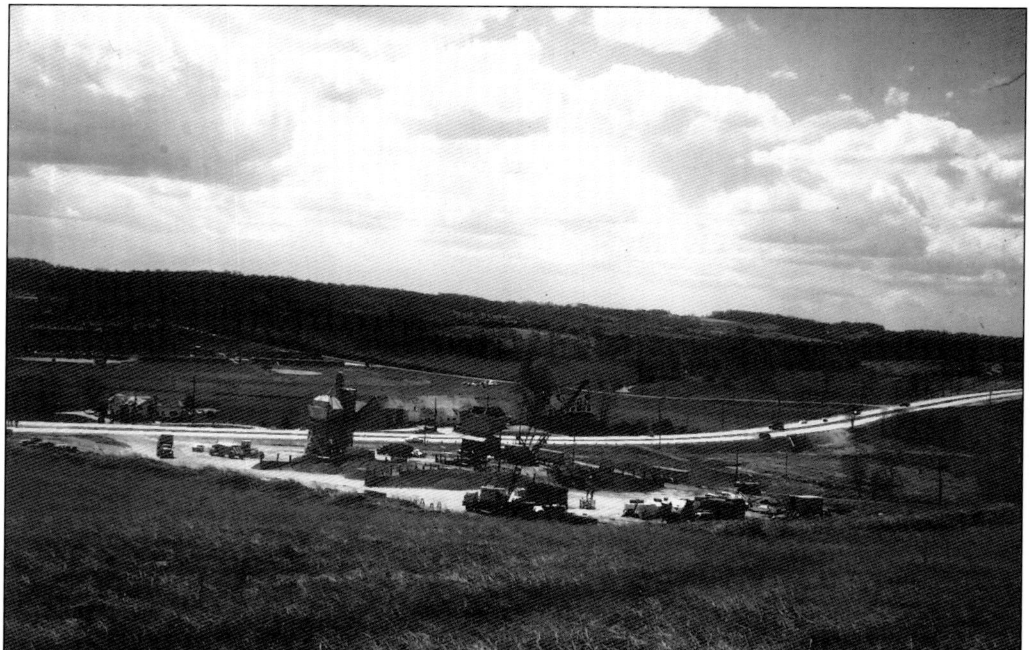

The growing amount of traffic along West Chester Pike to the burgeoning western suburbs of Philadelphia necessitated the removal of the trolley tracks and the widening of the highway in the mid-1950s. (Hilda Lucas.)

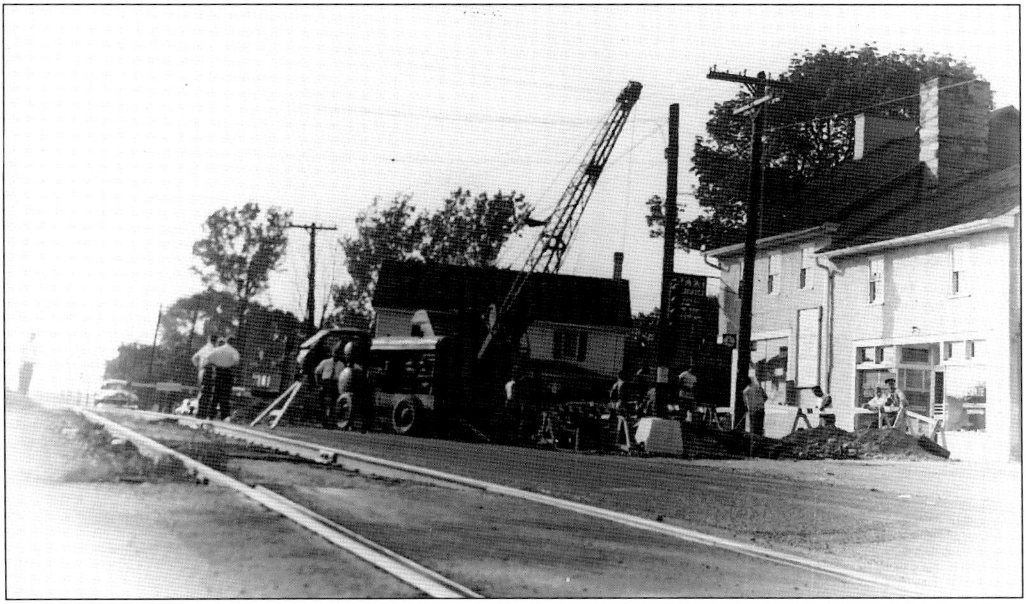

Crews demolish buildings during the widening of West Chester Pike in the mid-1950s. (Al Vandetty.)

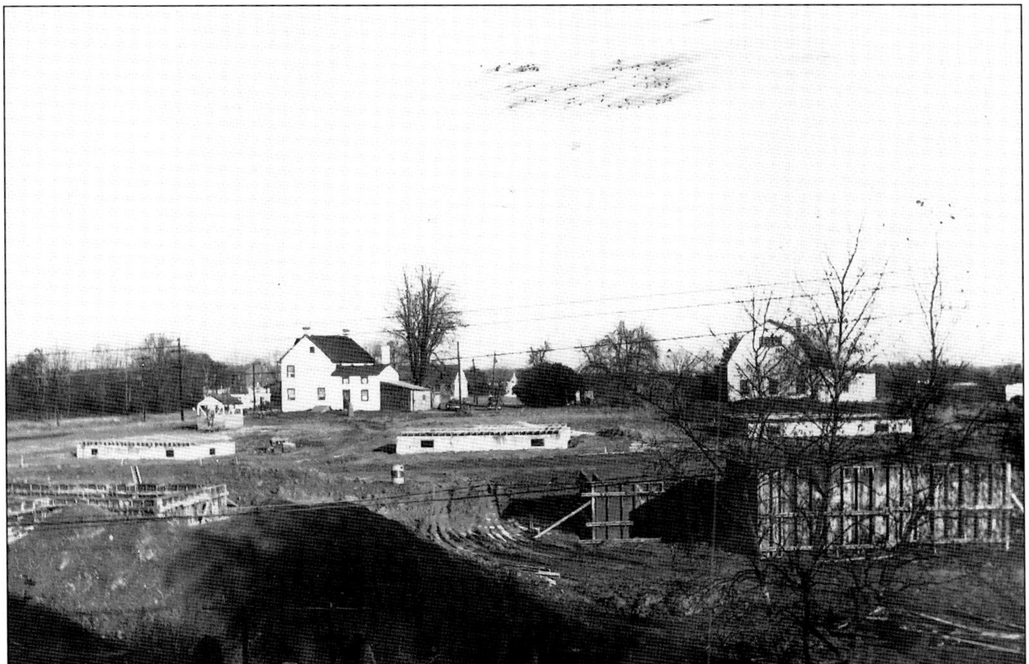

These farms in the area of West Greenhill Road would soon disappear as suburban sprawl marched westward. (Al Vandetty.)

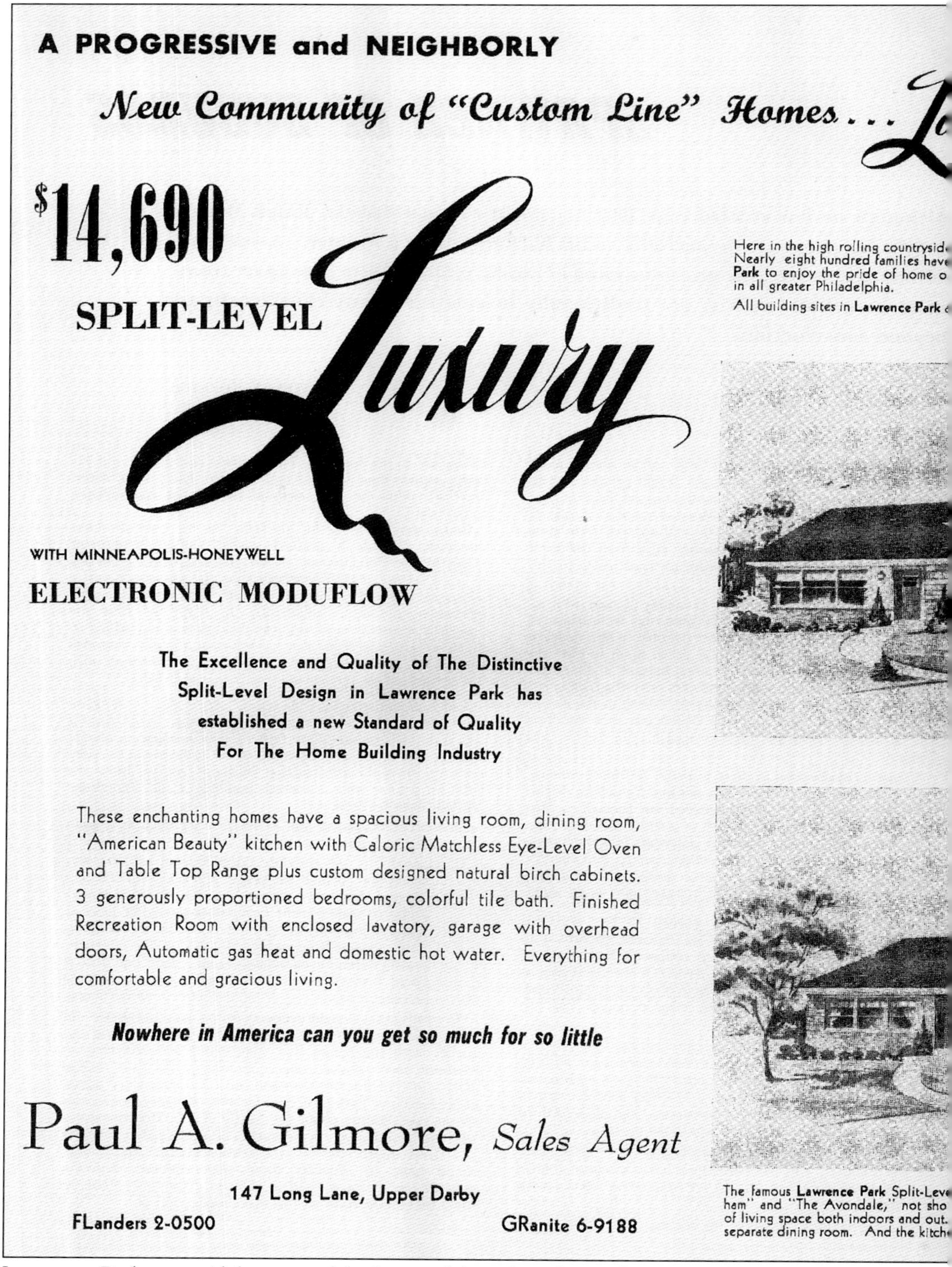

Lawrence Park was widely successful when it debuted in the mid-1950s with several styles of homes. The land on which the 1,200-home development was built was formerly owned by the

rple Township
Delaware County

he kind of people you will want for neighbors. here. People like you have come to **Lawrence** most progressive and desirable new community

for privacy, yet close enough for neighborliness.

stoga"

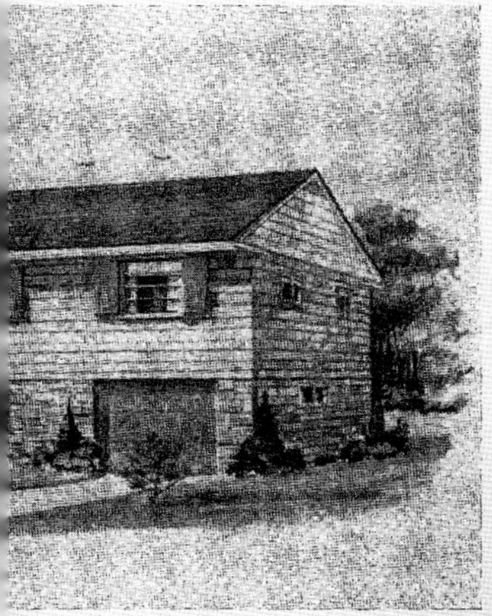

hester"

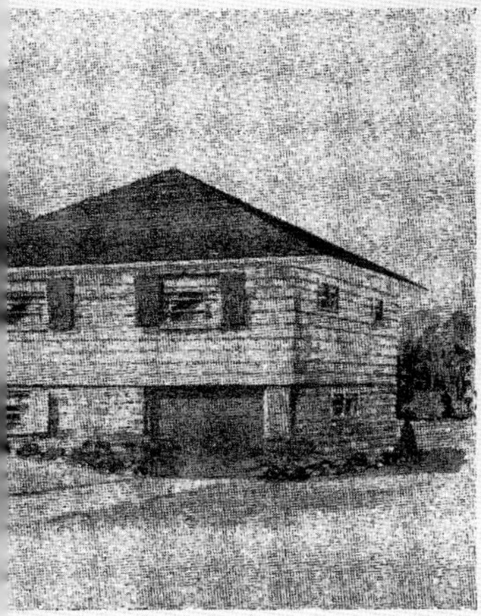

ered in four distinctive styles. "The Birming- y beautiful. Each provides an unusual amount ee spacious bedrooms; a big living room, and a verything you women ever hoped for, and more!

For outstanding design, modern construction features, finest quality at moderate cos

the name to remember **in home construction**

RALPH BODEK

Ralph Bodek

SUBURBAN PHILADELPHIA'S FOREMOST RESIDENTIAL DEVELOPER

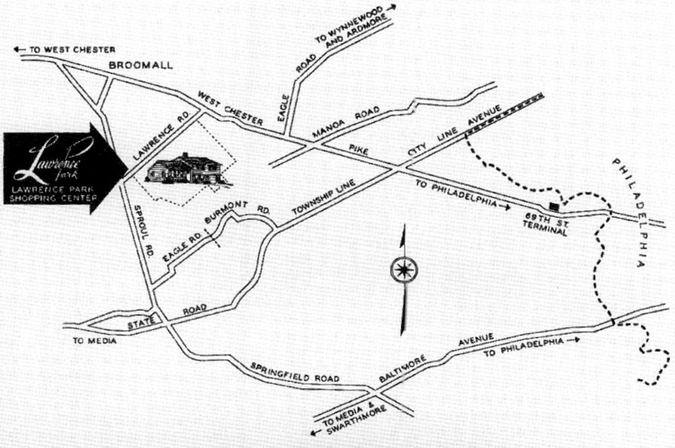

DIRECTIONS

- **From 69th & Market Sts., straight out West Chester Pike approximately 4½ miles to Lawrence Road in Broomall, turn left on Lawrence Road less than ½ mile to exhibit home.**
- **From Township Line and Sproul Road, west on Sproul Road approximately 2½ miles to Lawrence Road, turn right 1 mile to exhibit home.**
- **From 61st and Baltimore Ave., straight out Baltimore Pike to Sproul Road, turn right, continue about 3½ miles to Lawrence Road, turn right to exhibit home.**

Basic floor plan for the *famous* Lawrence Park homes.

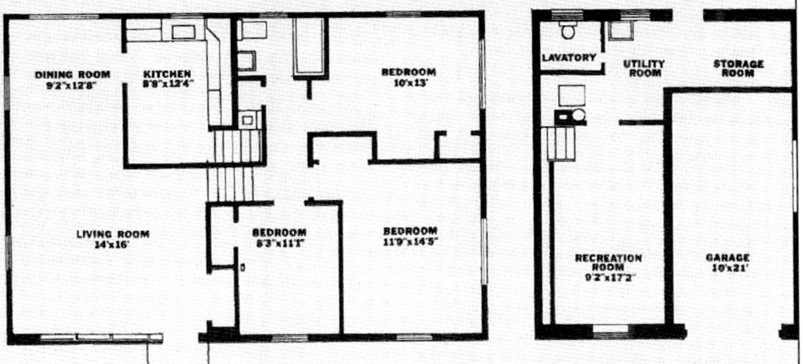

"the priceless ingredient in every home is the integrity of the builder"

president of American Markets, the predecessor of Acme. (Joe Bodek.)

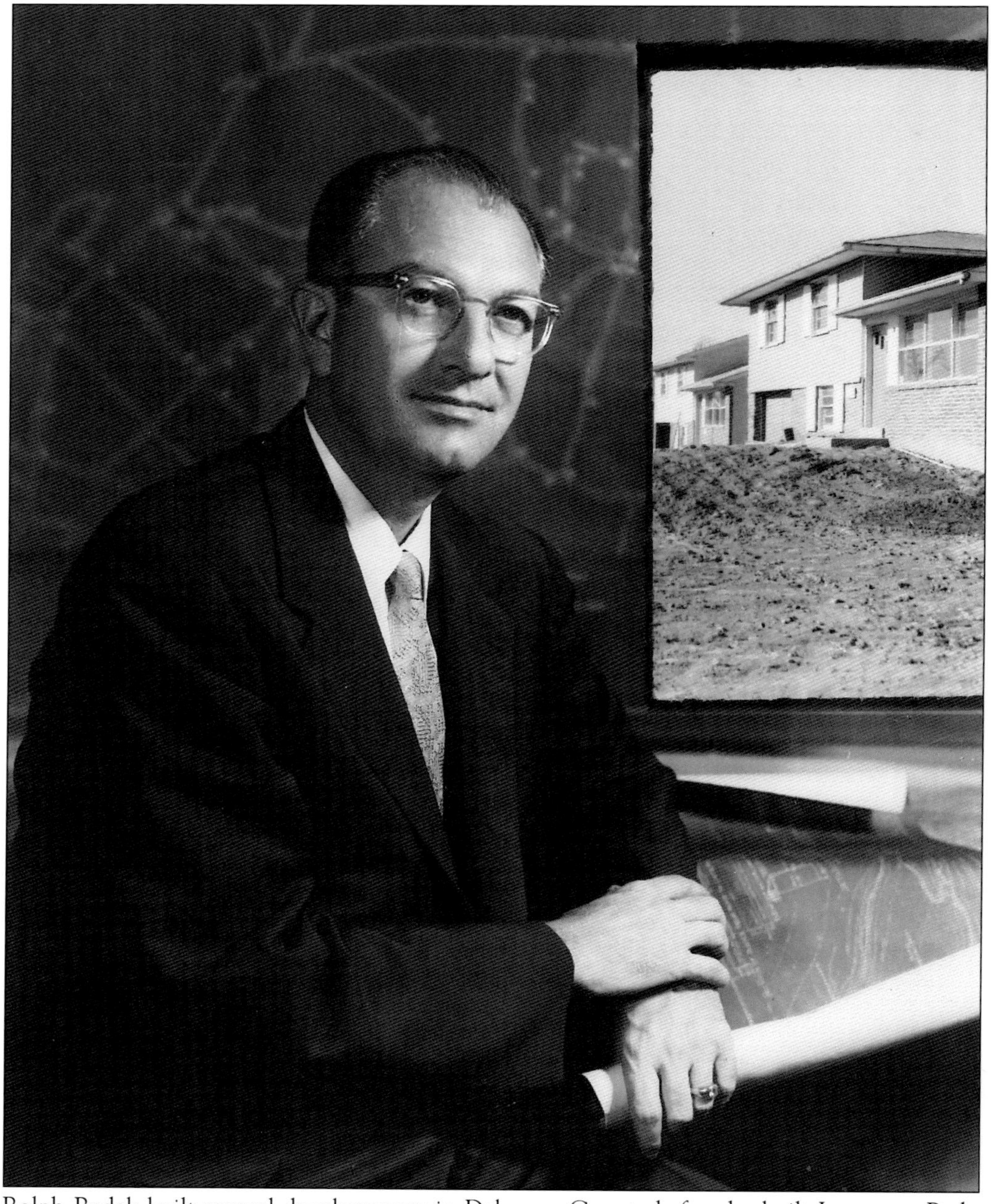

Ralph Bodek built several developments in Delaware County before he built Lawrence Park. He later moved to Florida, where he now lives and has developed commercial properties. (Joe Bodek.)

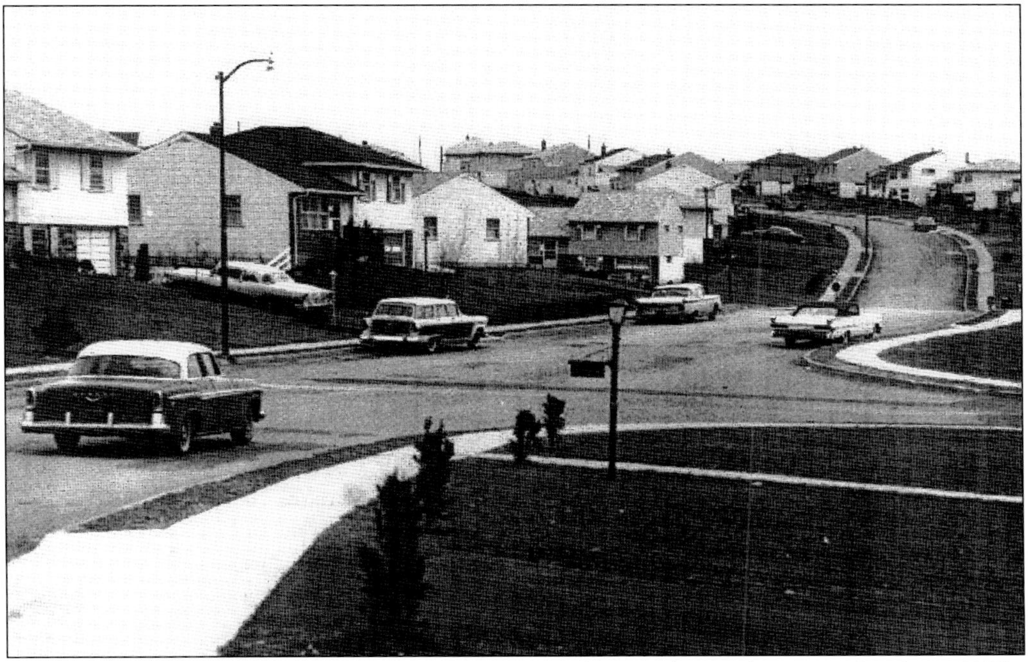

Parkway and Westbourne Drive in Lawrence Park are shown here in the late 1950s. (Hilda Lucas.)

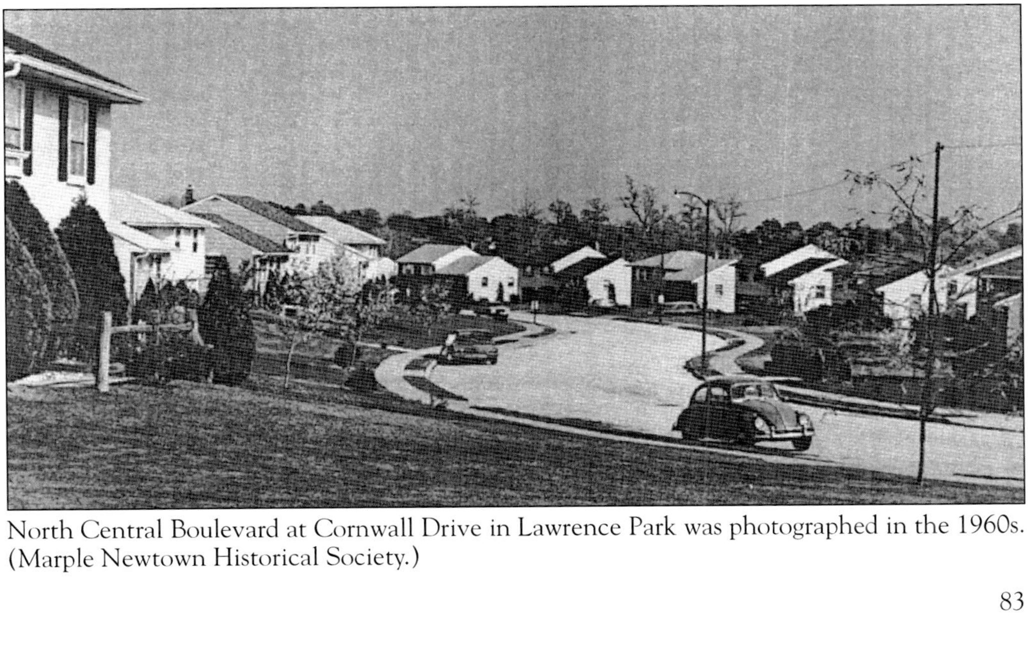

North Central Boulevard at Cornwall Drive in Lawrence Park was photographed in the 1960s. (Marple Newtown Historical Society.)

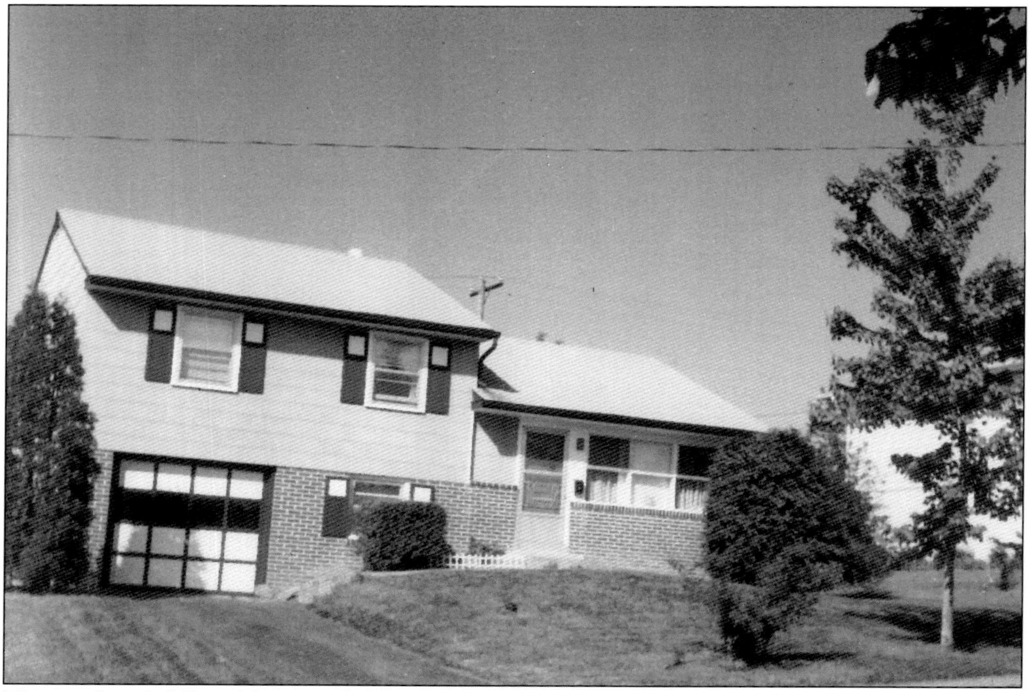

This is the childhood home of the author, 218 Cornwall Drive in Lawrence Park, in 1969. (Edward Mathis.)

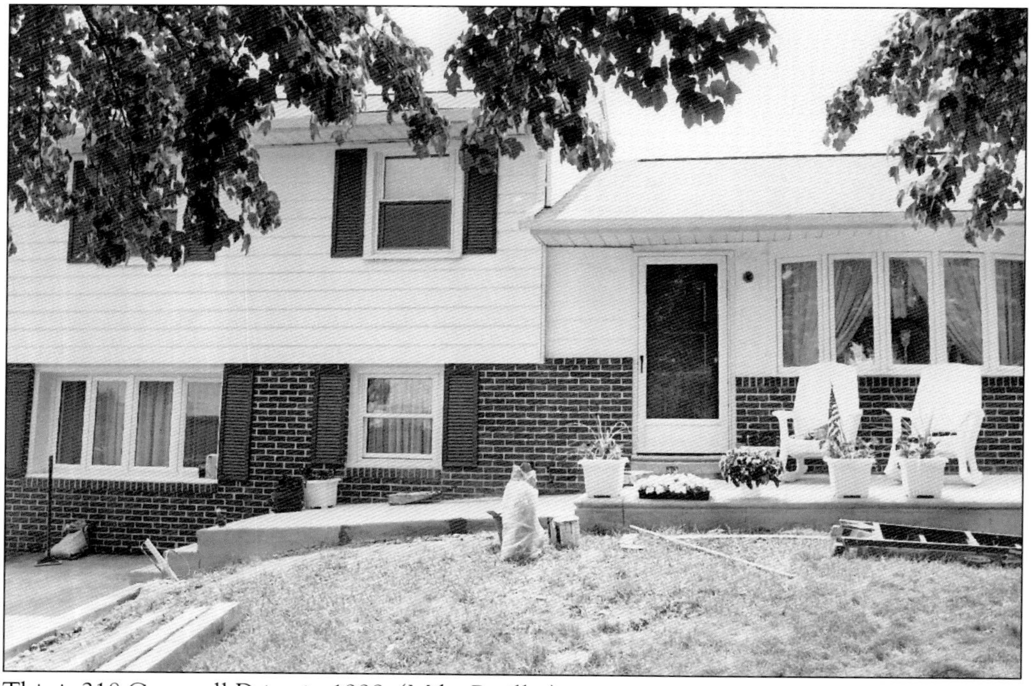

This is 218 Cornwall Drive in 1998. (Mike Perillo.)

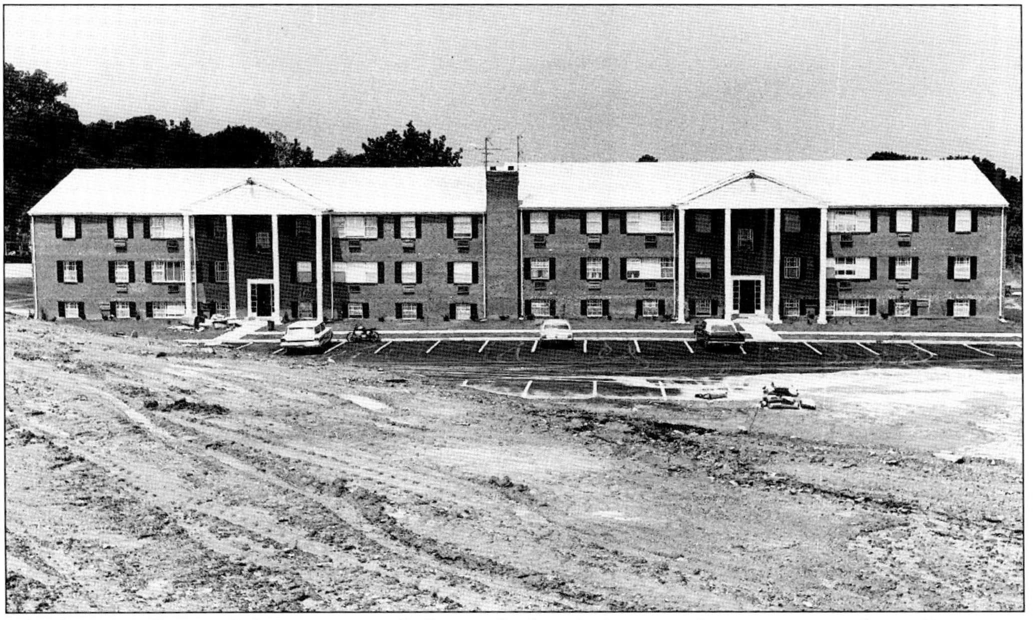

The housing boom did not just include single-family homes. Apartments such as Governor Sproul and the Evergreen Club Apartments also were built in the 1960s. (Frank Facciolo.)

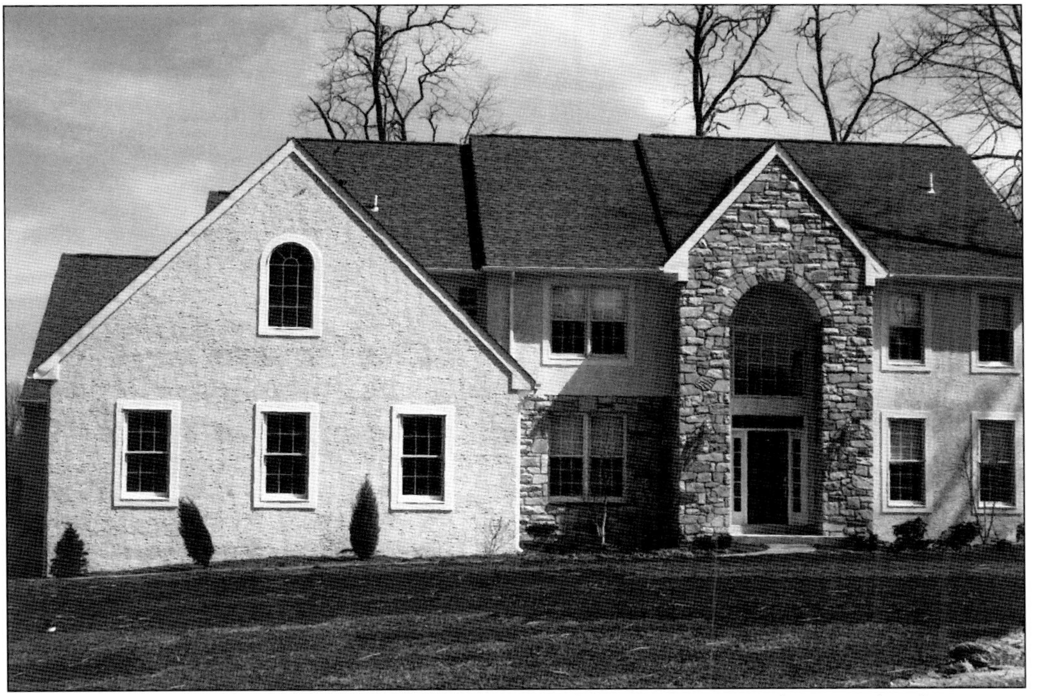

Since the early days of Ralph Bodek and Frank Facciolo, many expensive housing developments, some with price tags of up to $1 million, have been built in Marple and Newtown. This home, priced at $360,000, is located in The Woods at Langford development on Langford Road in Marple. (Mike Mathis.)

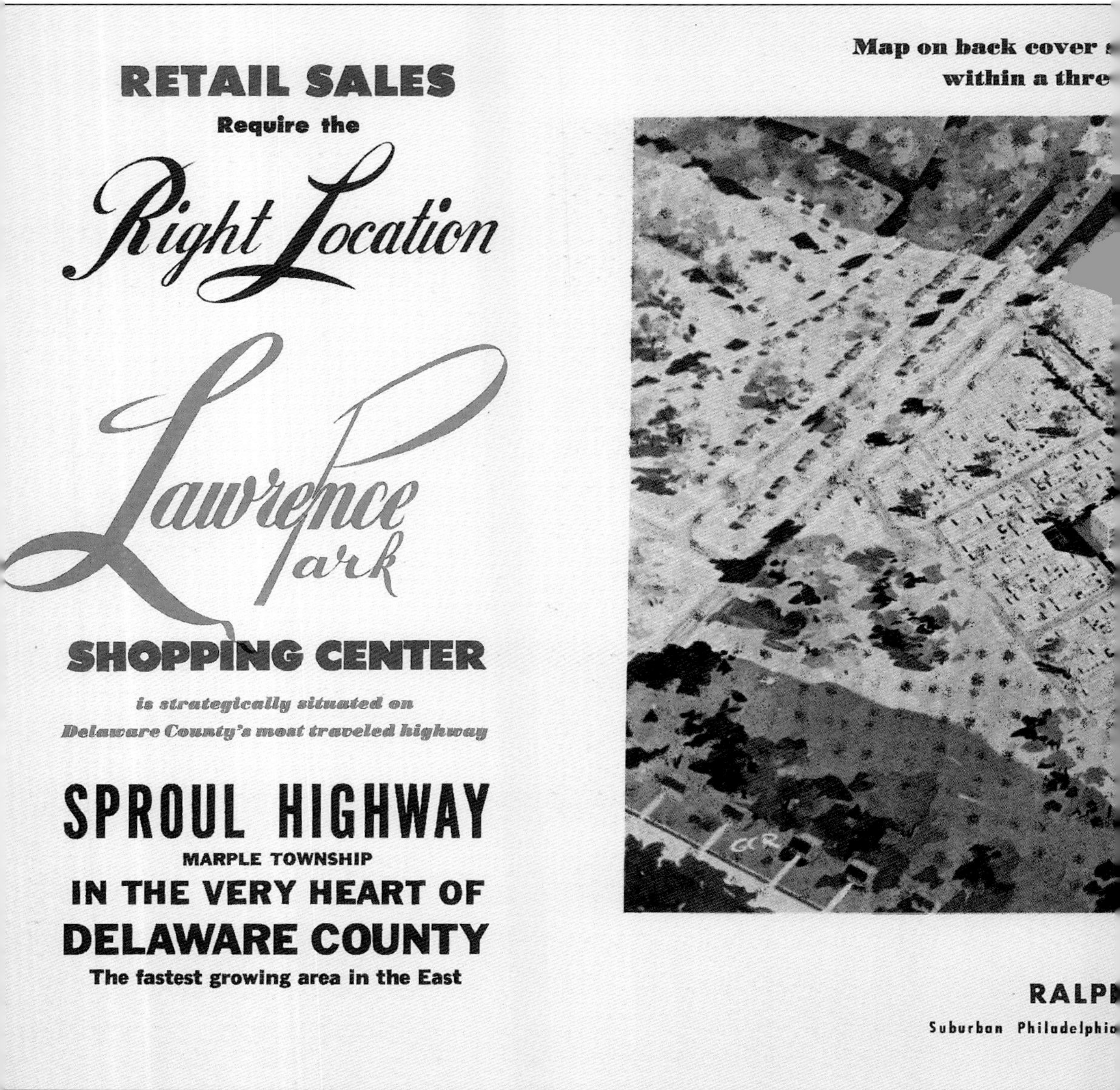

The Lawrence Park Shopping Center attracted such nationally known merchants as Grants and Woolworth as well as a movie theater and bowling alley. The Camera Shop and Alvin's Flower

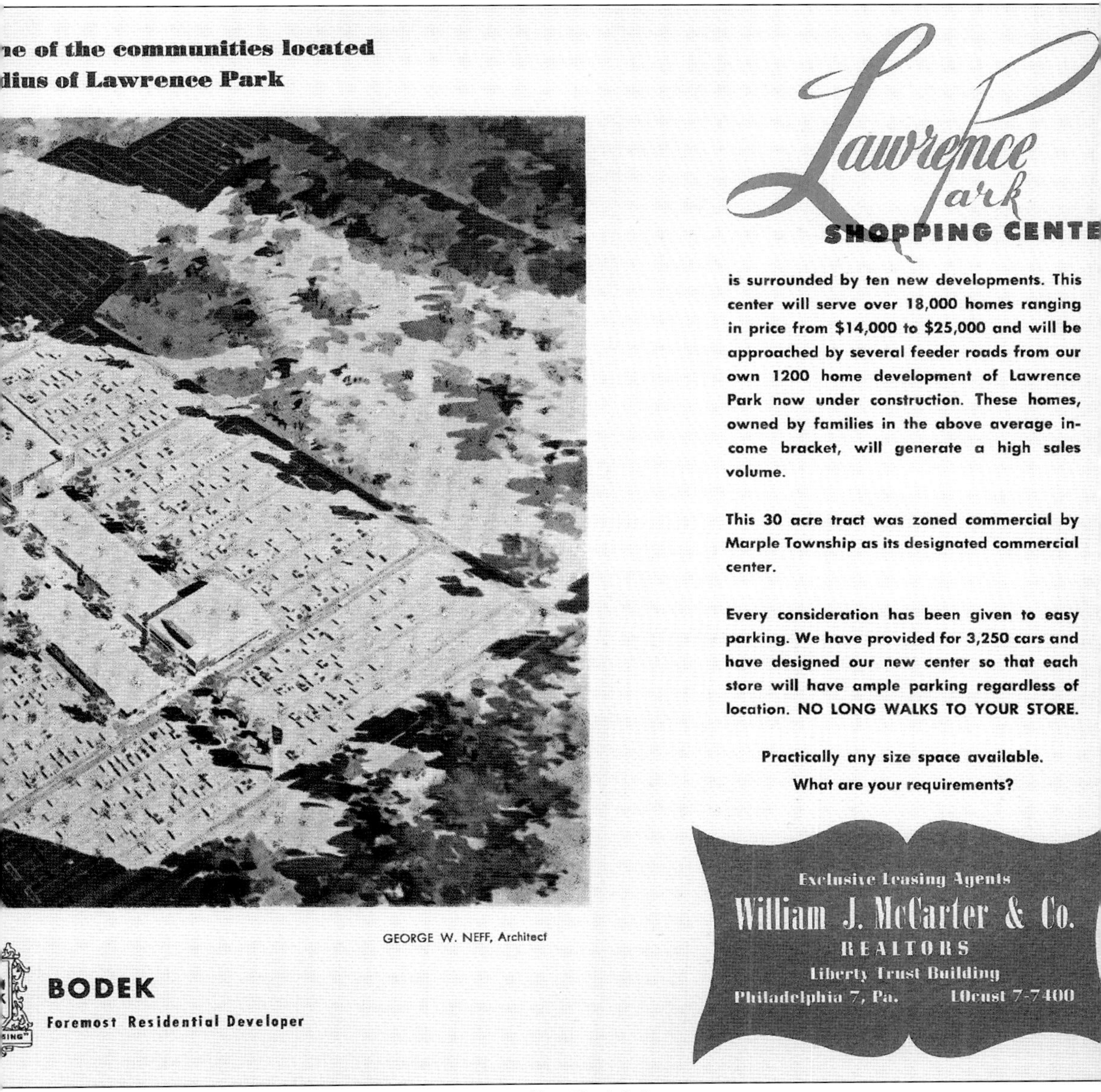

Shop are the only original remaining tenants. (Joe Bodek.)

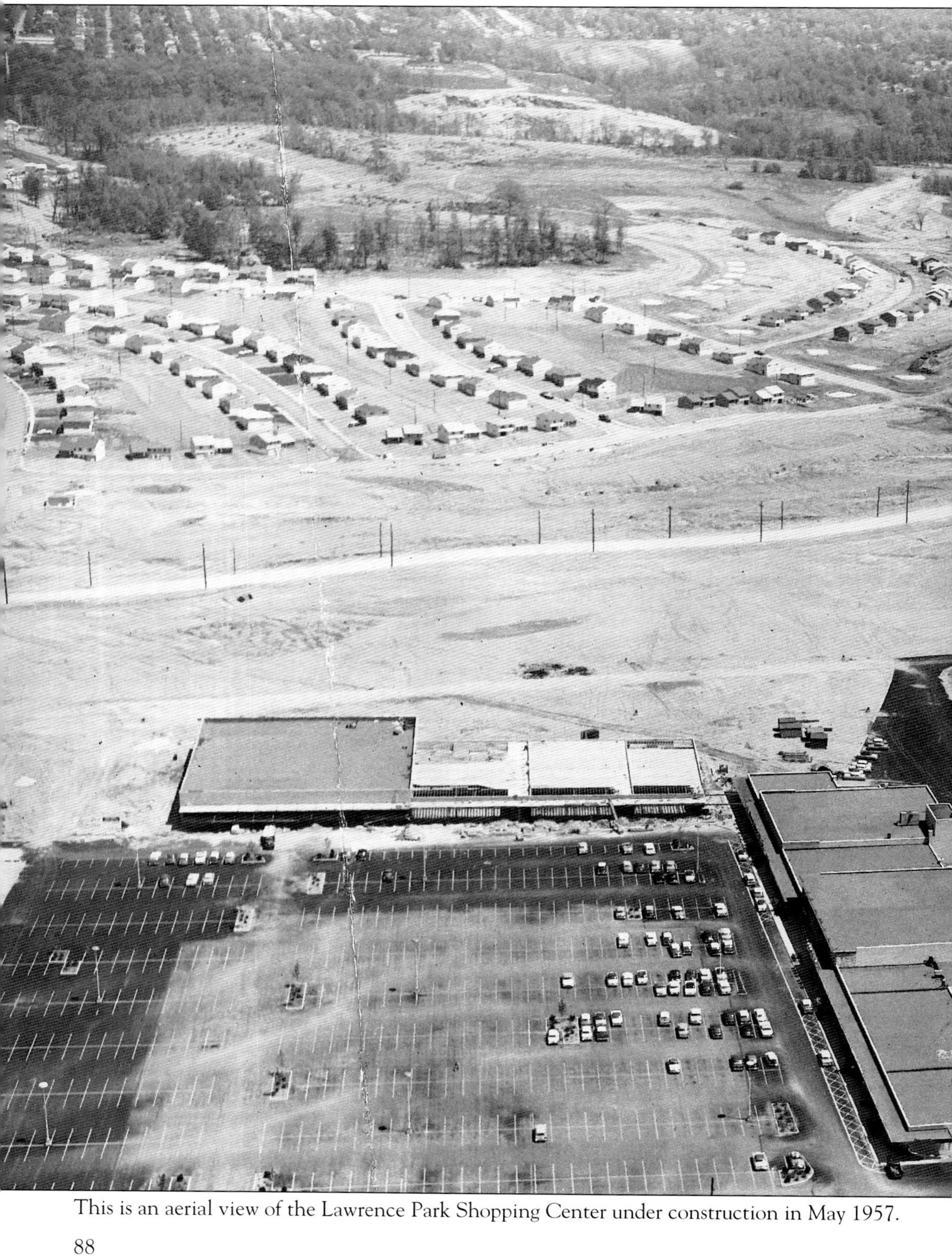

This is an aerial view of the Lawrence Park Shopping Center under construction in May 1957.

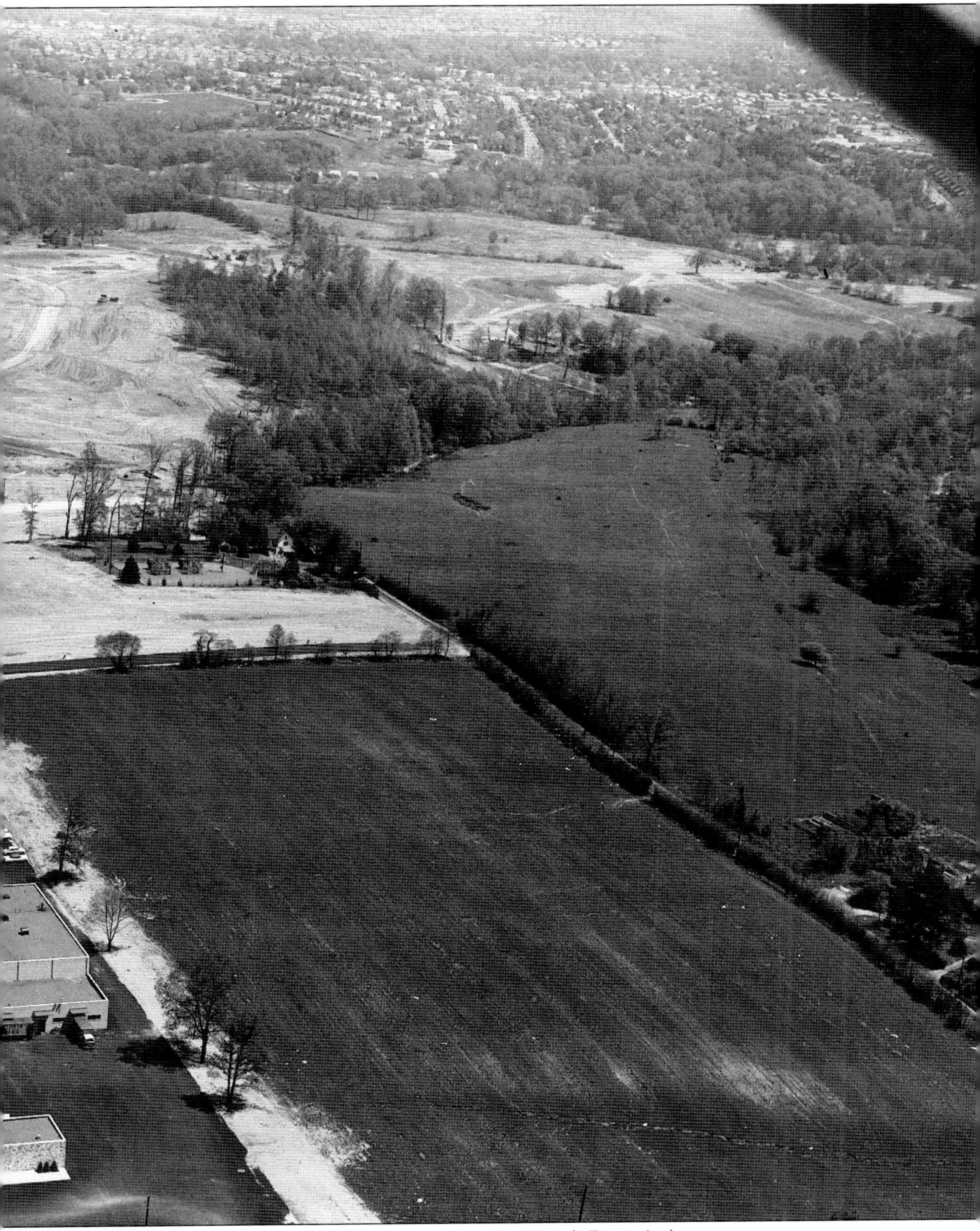

Homes under construction can be seen in the back. (Frank Facciolo.)

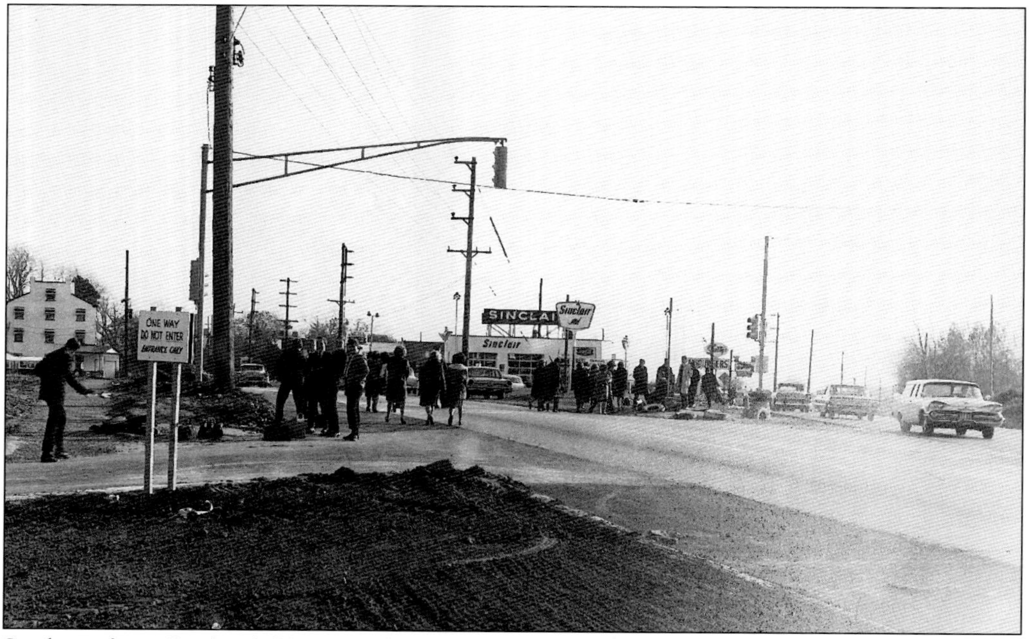

Students from Cardinal O'Hara walk across Springfield Road in the early 1960s. The Sinclair station later became Mike DiFurio's Exxon station, which was demolished to make way for the Blue Route. Scotty's hamburger stand was located behind the Sinclair station. (Marple Township Police Department.)

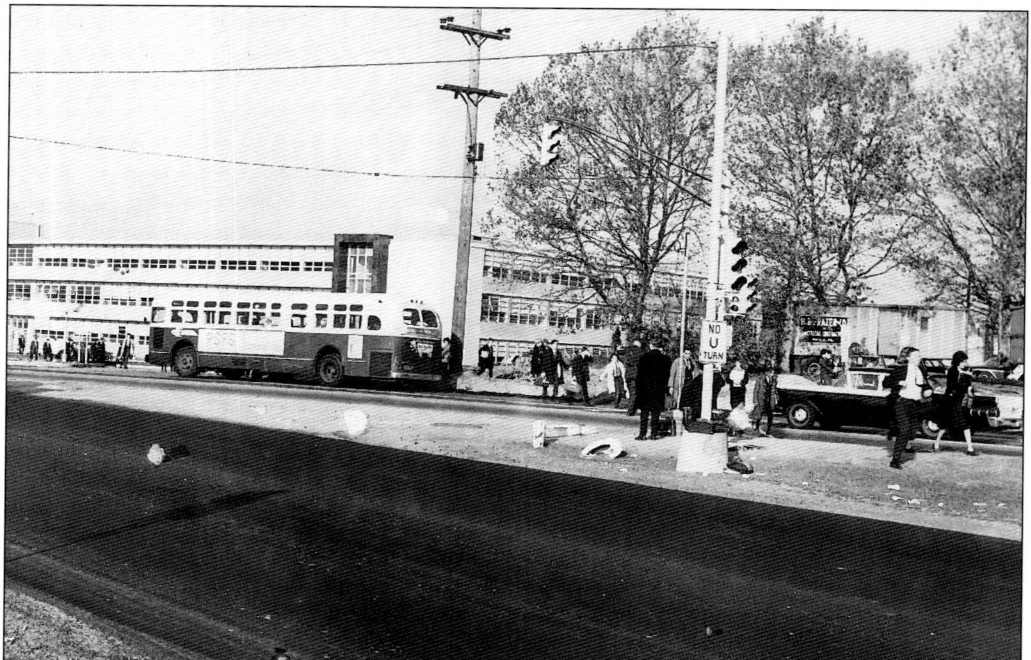

Buses and construction trailers parked outside Cardinal O'Hara High School are shown here just after its opening. (Marple Township Police Department.)

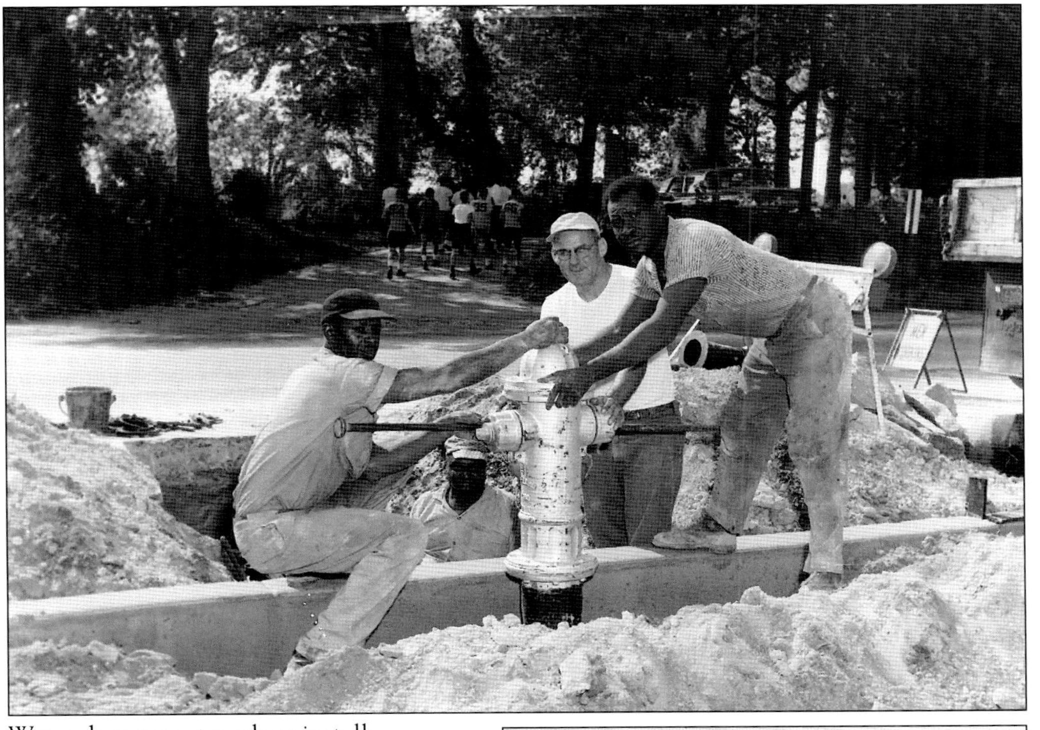

Water department workers install fire hydrants across from Cardinal O'Hara High School. (Marple Township Police Department.)

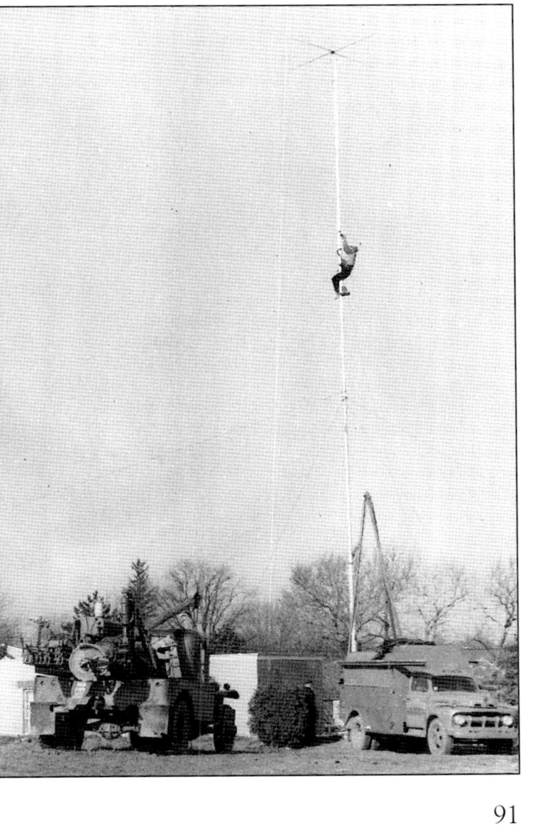

Workers install a new antenna outside the Marple Township Police Station. (Marple Township Police Department.)

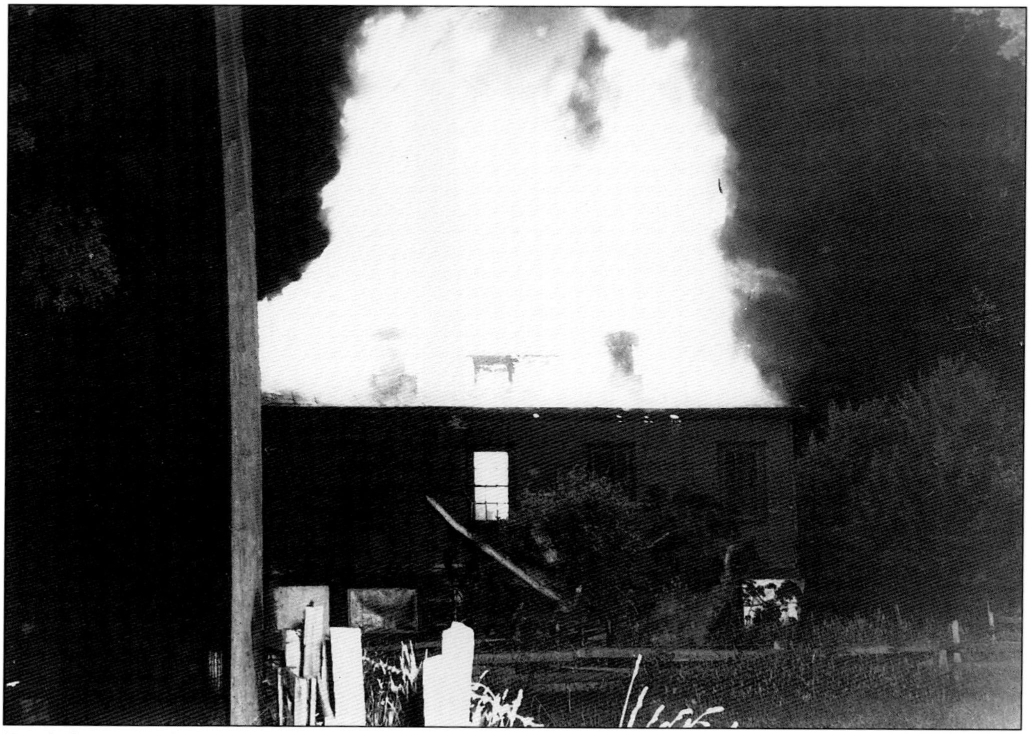

Firefighters work to extinguish a barn fire at Sproul and Old Marple Roads in July 1955. The barn was a remnant of a fast-disappearing rural lifestyle. (Marple Township Police Department.)

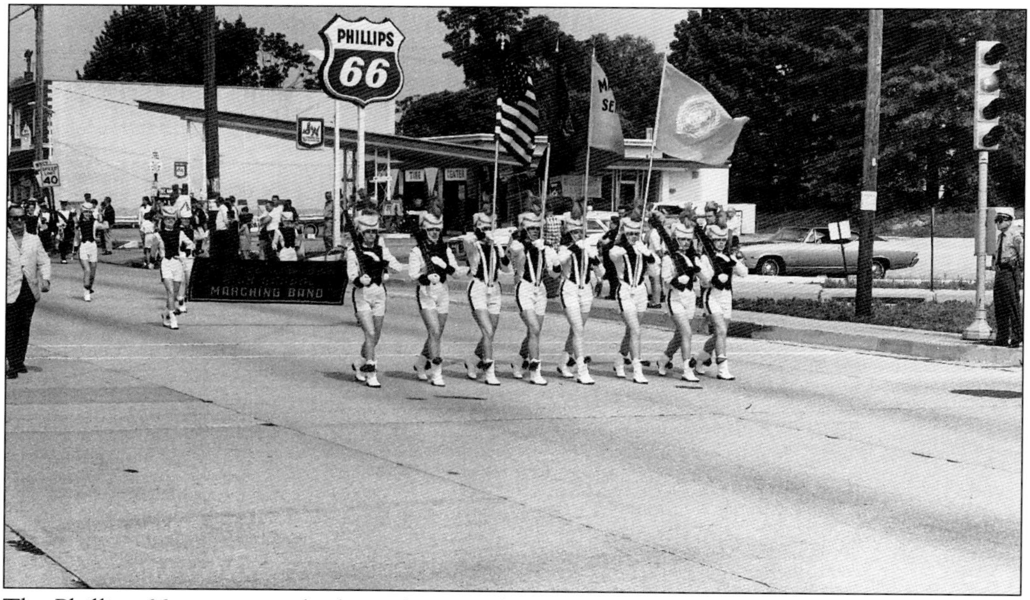

The Phillips 66 station was built on the site of Bonsall's store in the early 1960s to cater to the growing number of motorists in the area. It was torn down to make way for a steakhouse and is now the site of a McDonald's. (Bill Greco.)

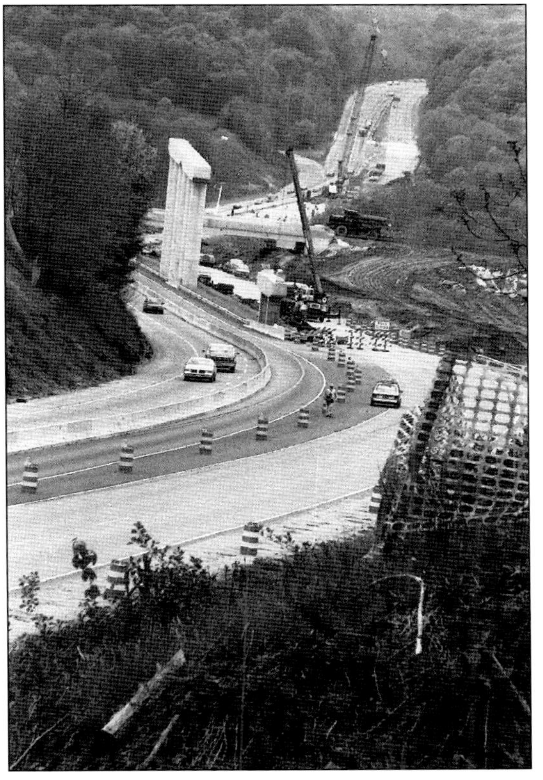

Construction of the Blue Route connecting Interstate 95 and the Pennsylvania Turnpike was proposed as early as the 1940s, but work did not begin until the 1990s. Here, the highway is being built at Route 1 and West Chester Pike. (*County Press.*)

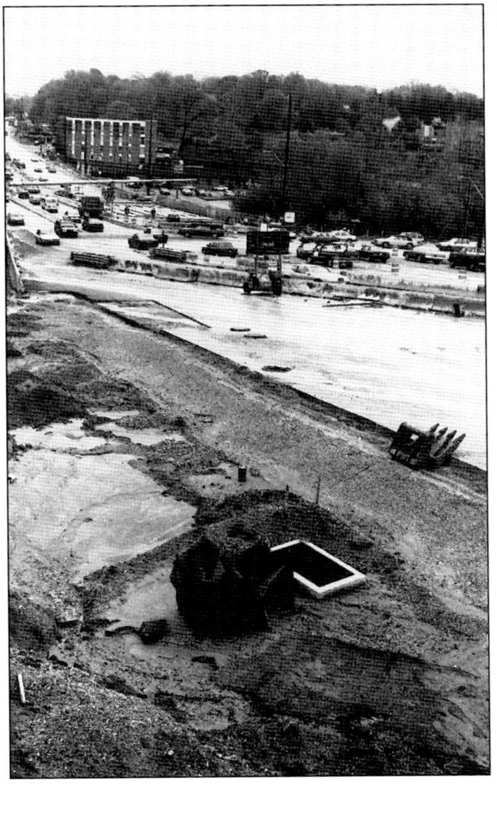

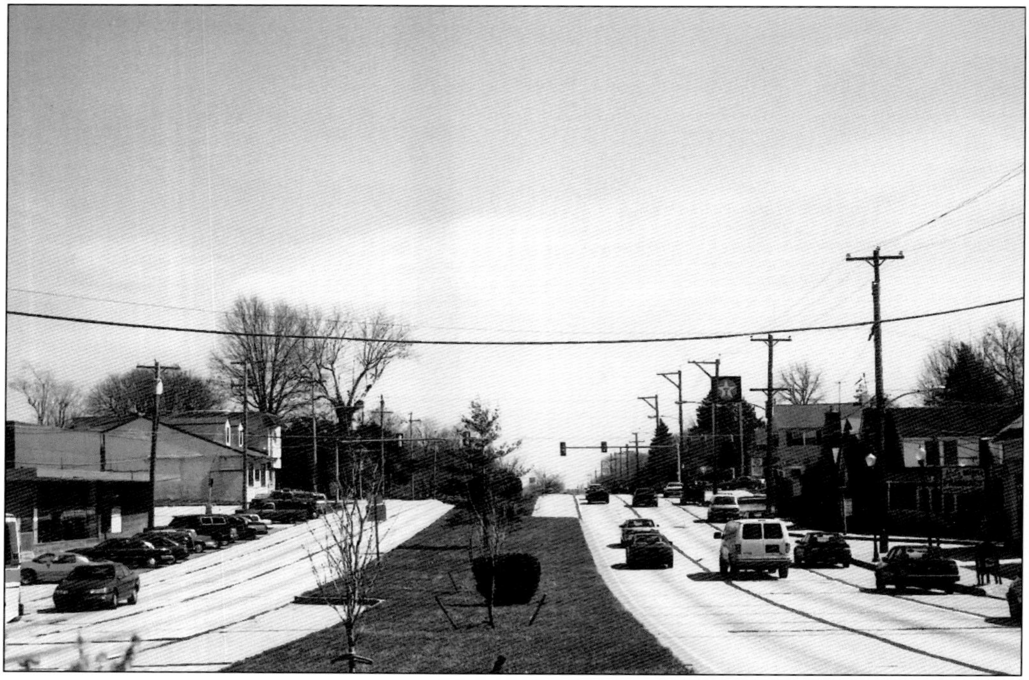

This is West Chester Pike in the Broomall business district looking east and west in 1998. (Mike Mathis.)

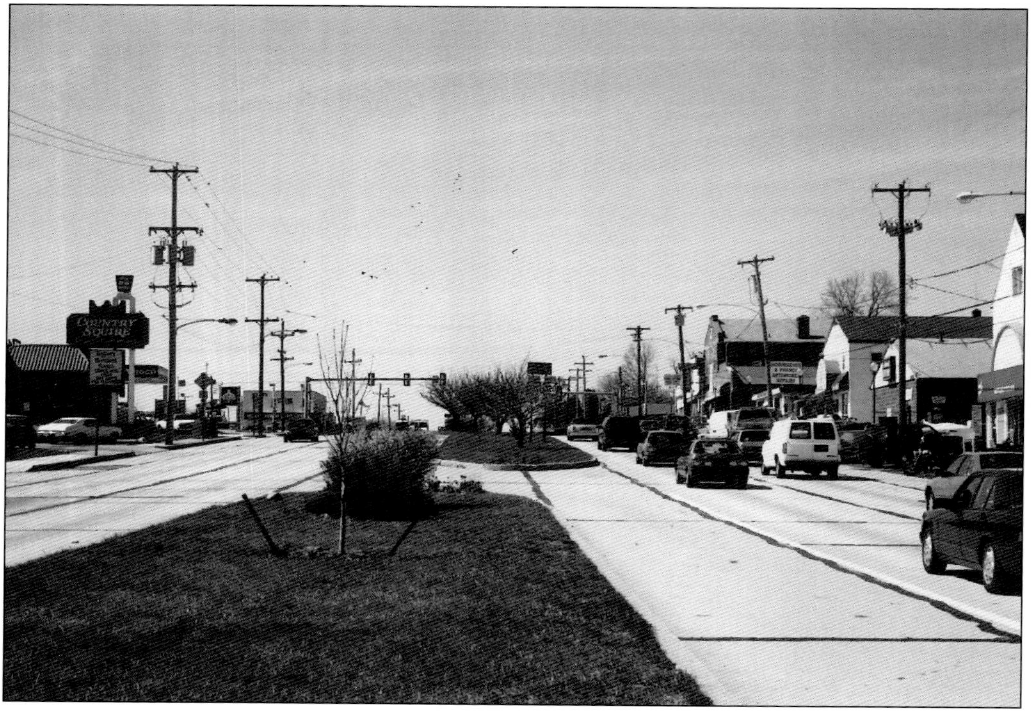

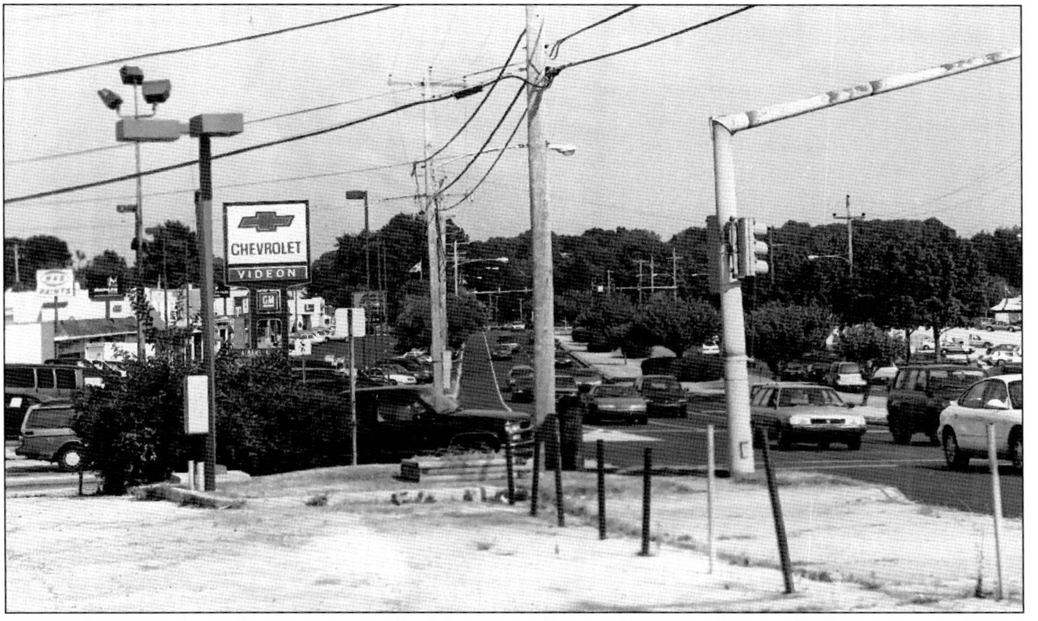

West Chester Pike is shown here in the Newtown Square business district looking east and west at Route 252 in 1998. (Mike Perillo.)

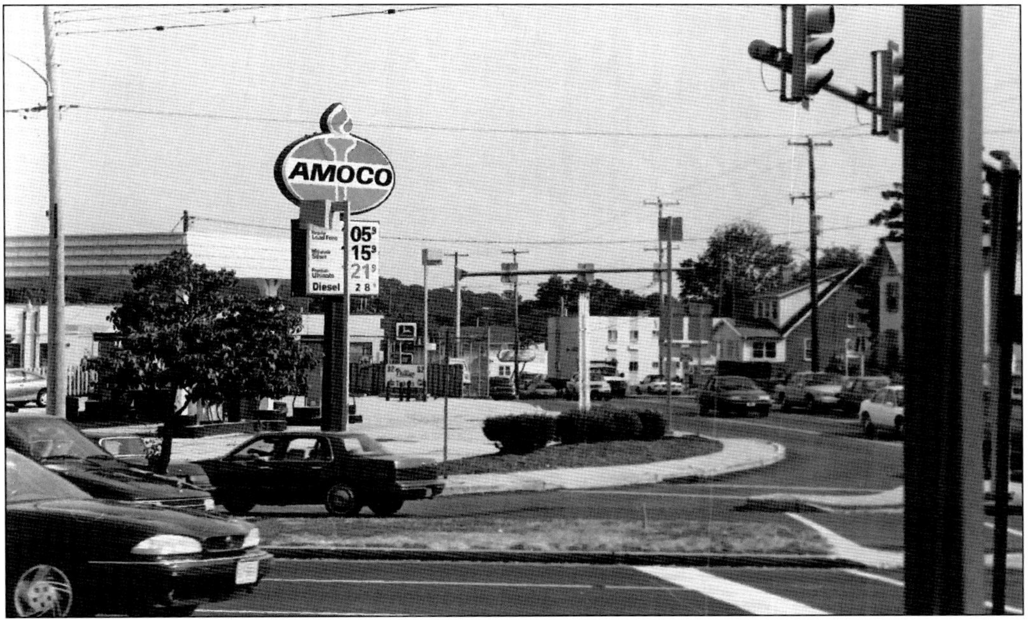

Acknowledgments

The following people were extremely helpful in compiling the photographs for this book: Rich Paul and Hilda Lucas of the Marple Newtown Historical Society, Richard Plotts, Seth Pancoast, Jan Ceton, Dick Standen, John Moyse, John Halota, Frank Facciolo, Joe Bodek, Vince Dortone, Al Vandetty, Mike Perillo, Pam Kitabjian, Bill Greco, John Kuseian, Pattie Price, Ed and Lucille Mathis, and the *County Press* newspaper.

I also want to thank my wife, Beverly, for her assistance, patience, and support during this project.

Bibliography

Alice and Carl Lindborg, Clara McVeigh, Erma Shaver, and others. *Historic Newtown Township, 1681–1983*. N.p.: Township of Newtown Tricentennial Commission, 1984.

Lucy Simler. *Marple Township: The First 100 Years*. N.p., n.d.